D0193249

BTEC FIRST AWARD

PUBLIC SERVICES

Debra Gray

ALWAYS LEARNING

PEARSON

Published by Pearson Education Limited, Edinburgh Gate, Harlow, Essex, CM20 2JE.
www.pearsonschoolsandfecolleges.co.uk
Text © Pearson Education Limited 2014
Typeset by Phoenix Photosetting, Chatham, Kent, UK
Original illustrations © Pearson Education Limited 2014
Illustrated by Phoenix Photosetting, Chatham, Kent, UK
Picture research by Rebecca Sodergren
Front cover photo © Getty Images: Monty Rakusen
Indexing by Torquil Harkness

The rights of Debra Gray to be identified as author of this work have been asserted by her in accordance with the Copyright, Designs and Patents Act 1988.

This edition published 2014.
18 17 16 15
10 9 8 7 6 5 4 3 2

British Library Cataloguing in Publication Data
A catalogue record for this book is available from the British Library

ISBN 978 1 446910 81 8

Copyright notice
All rights reserved. No part of this publication may be reproduced in any form or by any means (including photocopying or storing it in any medium by electronic means and whether or not transiently or incidentally to some other use of this publication) without the written permission of the copyright owner, except in accordance with the provisions of the Copyright, Designs and Patents Act 1988 or under the terms of a licence issued by the Copyright Licensing Agency, Saffron House, 6–10 Kirby Street, London EC1N 8TS (www.cla.co.uk). Applications for the copyright owner's written permission should be addressed to the publisher.

Printed in Slovakia by Neografia

Copies of official specifications for all Pearson qualifications may be found on: www.edexcel.com

A NOTE FROM THE PUBLISHER

In order to ensure that this resource offers high-quality support for the associated BTEC qualification, it has been through a review process by the awarding body to confirm that it fully covers the teaching and learning content of the specification or part of a specification at which it is aimed, and demonstrates an appropriate balance between the development of subject skills, knowledge and understanding, in addition to preparation for assessment.

While the publishers have made every attempt to ensure that advice on the qualification and its assessment is accurate, the official specification and associated assessment guidance materials are the only authoritative source of information and should always be referred to for definitive guidance.

BTEC examiners have not contributed to any sections in this resource relevant to examination papers for which they have responsibility.

No material from an endorsed book will be used verbatim in any assessment set by BTEC.

Endorsement of a book does not mean that the book is required to achieve this BTEC qualification, nor does it mean that it is the only suitable material available to support the qualification, and any resource lists produced by the awarding body shall include this and other appropriate resources.

Picture Credits

The publisher would like to thank the following for their kind permission to reproduce their photographs:

(Key: b-bottom; c-centre; l-left; r-right; t-top)

Alamy Images: BlueMoon Stock 157, Kevin Britland 101, Mia Caruana 99, Hot Shots 45, Alun Jenkins 153, Justin Kase zfivez 103, Ilene MacDonald 133, Martin Phelps 3, Radharc Images 122; **Corbis:** Philip Lee Harvey / Cultura 129, Robert Michael 43, Reuters / Darren Staples 69, Toby Melville / Reuters 112, Brian Stewart / Epa 5; **Crown Copyright 2014:** 8, 31, 54, 76, 90; **Crown Copyright Courtesy of the Department of Health in association with the Welsh Government, the Scottish Government and the Food Standards Agency in Northern Ireland:** 140; **Kelly Stevens:** 37; **Getty Images:** Popperfoto 6; **Pearson Education Ltd:** Jon Barlow 102, Naki Kouyioumtzis 33; **Press Association Images:** Peter Macdiarmid 71; **Rex Features:** 80, Aflo 116, Global Warming Images 131, Janine Wiedel 67; **Shutterstock.com:** CatonPhoto U1-banner, CREATISTA 100, Darrenp U3-banner, Gstock studio 65, Lenar Musin 50b, Dino Osmic 137; **SuperStock:** BreBa / Beyond U2-banner; **Veer / Corbis:** Bike World Travel 22, Dmitry Kalinovsky 151, Flashon 50t, Warren Goldswain 2, Robert Kneschke 160, Elinna Mannien 44, Martinan 132, Matthew Ragen U5-banner, PT Images 130, RNI 68, Ron from York 106, Sam74100 66, Tom Gowanlock U4-banner, Rui Vale de Sousa 42, Willaim 87, 147.

All other images © Pearson Education

Every effort has been made to trace the copyright holders and we apologise in advance for any unintentional omissions. We would be pleased to insert the appropriate acknowledgement in any subsequent edition of this publication.

Data sources

© Crown Copyright, contains public sector information licensed under the Open Government Licence v2.0: p.7, data on Fire and Rescue authorities from the Department for Communities and Local Government (*Fire and Rescue Operational Statistics Bulletin for England 2012–13*); p.7, data on ambulance response times from Department of Health (www.nhs.uk); p.8, armed services employment figures from the Ministry of Defence (*UK Armed Forces Annual Personnel Report*, 1 Apr 2013 and www.gov.uk); p.9, British Army employment figures from Ministry of Defence (*Transforming the British Army*, Jul 2013); p.12, local government employment figures from the Department for Local Government and Communities (*Local Government Financial Statistics England, No.23*, May 2013); p.19, NHS employment data and NHS budget information from Department of Health (www.nhs.uk); p.19, information about obesity and alcohol-related hospital admissions from Department of Health (www.nhs.uk); p.28, information about partnership delivery of health care from UK Trade and Investment, Department of Health and NHS (*Healthcare UK: Public Private Partnerships*); p.30, Police Service budgets from the Home Office (*The Police Grant Report (England and Wales) 2013/14*); p.31, data on corporation tax from HM Revenue and Customs (*Corporation Tax Statistics*, 31 Oct 2013); p.56, data on ambulance trusts from Department of Health (www.nhs.uk); p.57, information about Crown Censures from www.hse.gov.uk; p.74, definition of major incident from Civil Contingencies Act 2004; p.77, Civil Service employment figures Civil Service from www.ons.gov.uk (*Civil Service Statistics*, 2013); p.77, Police Service employment figures from the Home Office (*Statistics – Police workforce, England and Wales*, 31 Mar 2013); p.80, armed services employment figures from Ministry of Defence (*UK Armed Forces, Annual Personnel Report*, 1 Apr 2013 and *Human resources for civilians working for the Ministry of Defence*, 24 Jan 2013); pp.81–2, information on infantry soldier role, mine warfare specialist role and nursing officer role from Ministry of Defence; p.83, information on police constable role from Home Office; p.85, information on ambulance care assistant role from www.nhscareers. nhs.uk; p.85, information on police community support officer role from Home Office; p.91, information about the Police Service and Royal Navy application processes from Home Office and Ministry of Defence; p.94, information about the Royal Navy application process from Ministry of Defence; p.97, information about Army starting salaries from Ministry of Defence; p.113, racist incident figures from Home Office, Ministry of Justice and Office of National Statistics (*An Overview of Hate Crime in England and Wales*, Dec 2013); p.121, crime statistics from Office of National Statistics (Statistical Bulletin *Crime in England and Wales, Year Ending September 2013*, 23 Jan 2014); p.121, data on child poverty from Department of Work and Pensions and Office of National Statistics (*Households Below Average Income: An analysis of the income distribution 1994/95 – 2011/12*, Jun 2013); p.121, data on pensioners on low incomes from Department for Work and Pensions (*Understanding pensioner poverty and material deprivation*, Research Report 827, Feb 2013); p.121, data on disabled hate crime from Crown Prosecution Service (*Policy for Prosecuting Cases of Disability Hate Crime*, Feb 2007); p.121, data on disabilities from Department for Work and Pensions; p.125, data on workplace accidents from HSE (*Key annual figures 2012/13*); p.126, cadet force figures from Ministry of Defence (*TSP7 – UK Reserve Forces and Cadets*, 1 Apr 2013); p.128, data on child protection plans from Department for Education and Office of National Statistics (*SFR45/2013 Characteristics of Children in Need in England, 2012–13*, 31 Oct 2013); p.129, figures on magistrates from Ministry of Justice; p.129, data about waste from Department for Environment, Food & Rural Affairs; p.131, data on road accidents from Department for Transport (*Reported Road Casualties in Great Britain: Main Results 2012*, 27 Jun 2013); pp.140–142, information about vitamins and minerals from Department of Health (www.nhs.uk); p.146, data on poverty in UK from Department for Work and Pensions (*Households below average income (HBAI)*, 29 Apr 2014); p.148, data on obesity from Department of Health (www.nhs.uk); p.149, data on high blood pressure from Department of Health (www.nhs.uk); p.153, data on smoking-related deaths and smoking-related heart disease from Department of Health (www.nhs.uk); p.158, information on HM Prison Service fitness tests from Ministry of Justice; pp.158–159, information on the Potential Royal Marines Course (PRMC) from Ministry of Defence; p.164, information about BMI ranges from Department of Health (www.nhs.uk).

© Parliamentary Copyright, contains Parliamentary information licensed under the Open Parliament Licence v1.0: p.9, Royal Navy and Royal Air Force employment figures from House of Commons Library Standard Note SN/SG/02183 (*Defence personnel statistics*, 19 Sep 2013); p.15, data on domestic abuse from House of Commons Library Standard Note SN/HA/6337 (*Domestic Violence*, 23 Dec 2013); p.86, PCSO figures from House of Commons Library Standard Note SN00634 (*Police service strength*, 25 Jul 2013); p.93, Police Service employment figures from House of Commons Library Standard Note SN00634 (*Police service strength*, 25 Jul 2013); p.128, data on special constable figures from House of Commons Library Standard Note SN00634 (*Police service strength*, 25 Jul 2013).

Author's acknowledgements – thanks to:

South Yorkshire Fire and Rescue Service
Derbyshire Fire and Rescue Service
South Yorkshire Police
Derbyshire Constabulary
East Midlands Ambulance Service

The public service teams and students at Dearne Valley College, Chesterfield College, Henley College Coventry and Grimsby Institute of Further and Higher Education

L/Cpl Kelly Stevens 38 Signals Regiment

Neil Carruthers – Mountain Rescue

Tim Binns
Stefan Fusenich
Special Constable Jason Pimborough
Tez Gittens

Ben, India, Sam and Genevieve for all the cups of tea and patience.

This book is designed to help you through your BTEC First in Public Services, and covers five units of the qualification.

▶ About your BTEC First in Public Services

Choosing to study a BTEC First Public Services qualification is a great decision to make for lots of reasons. The public services sector covers a variety of areas, and offers a huge choice of careers. So, whether you want to be an ambulance driver, a housing officer in your local authority or someone who works with charitable organisations, a BTEC First Public Services qualification can help you to get one step closer to achieving your goal. Your BTEC will give you an insight into the breadth of this sector as well as sharpening your skills to prepare you for employment or further study.

▶ About the author

Debra Gray has taught public services in the further education sector for over 18 years. She has a degree in Criminology and masters degrees in Criminal Justice and Education Management. She has written numerous publications for both learners and tutors across a range of public services qualifications over the last 14 years. Debra has also served as an HMI (Her Majesty's Inspector) for Ofsted. She is currently Deputy Principal of a large Further Education college.

This book is designed to help you use your skills and knowledge in work-related situations, and to assist you in getting the most from your course.

These introductions give you a snapshot of what to expect from each unit – and what you should be aiming for by the time you finish it.

How this unit is assessed

Learning aims describe what you will be doing in the unit.

A learner shares their experience of working through the unit.

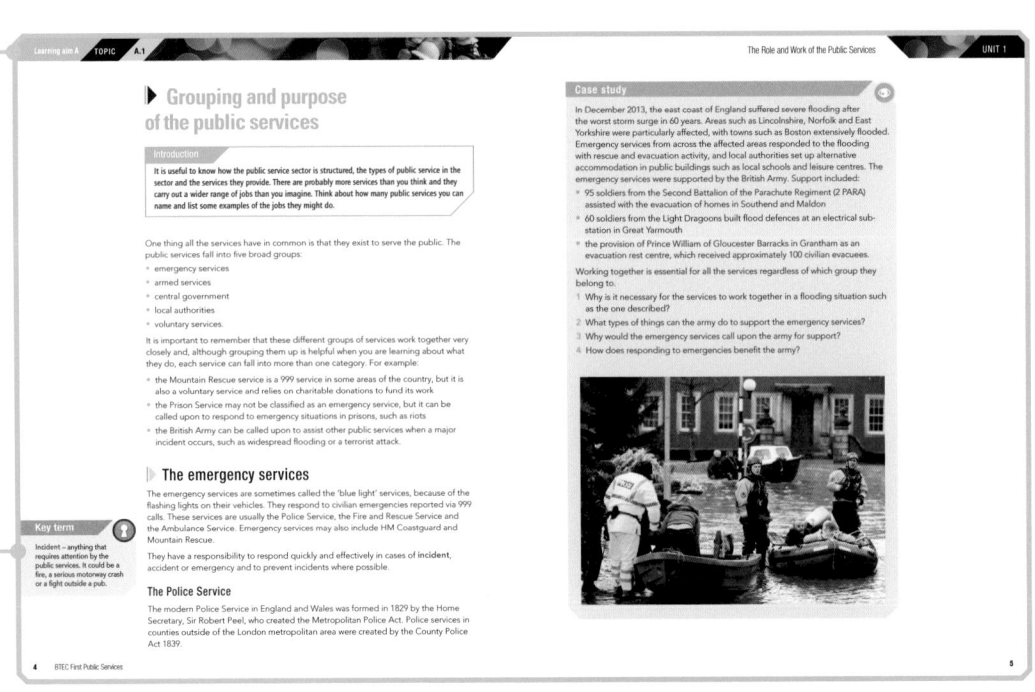

Features of this book

There are lots of features in this book to help you learn about the topics in each unit, and to have fun while learning! These pages show some of the features that you will come across when using the book.

Learning aim and topic references show which parts of your BTEC you are covering.

Key terms are important words or phrases that you will come across. Key terms appear in blue bold text and are defined within the topic or in a key terms box on the page. Also see the glossary.

Activity 1.4 — Communication in the armed services

Like the emergency services, the armed services also need to be able to communicate effectively with each other. Can you think of five reasons why this is important?

Activities will help you to learn about the topic. They can be completed in pairs or groups, or sometimes on your own.

Assessment practice 1.1

1 Identify two armed service reserves. [2]
2 Identify the three main functions of the armed services. [3]
3 Explain how the armed service reserves work with their regular counterparts. [2]

A chance to practise answering the types of test questions that you may come across in the paper-based examination. (For Unit 1 only.)

Assessment activity 2.2 — *English*

To show you can work as part of a team, you will take part in two teamwork activities:

1 simulated communications exercise using radios or non-verbal communications
2 fire safety campaign designed to prevent young people making hoax calls to the Fire and Rescue Service.

You need to play a different role in each scenario and act positively as a member of the team, demonstrating your teamwork skills. At the end, you need to consider your own performance as part of the team, thinking about what your strengths were and what you can do to develop an action plan to overcome your weaknesses.

Tips

- Try to play an active part in the simulation to show your effective teamwork skills.
- Be honest about what went well and what you need to do to improve.

Activities that relate to the unit's assessment criteria. These activities will help you prepare for your assignments and contain tips to help you achieve your potential. (For all units **except** Unit 1.)

Just checking

1 What is a major incident?
2 List three types of major incident.
3 Identify three things that need to happen at the scene of a major incident.

Use these questions to check your knowledge and understanding of the topic you have just covered.

Someone who works in the public services sector explains how this unit of the BTEC First applies to the day-to-day work they do as part of their job.

WorkSpace

Lance Corporal Kelly Stevens

Army Reserve

I work as part of 38 Signals Regiment, which is an Army Reserve regiment with responsibility for providing information and communication systems to the emergency services and local government in an emergency. We can also be deployed overseas with regular soldiers. We can be called upon to do a variety of things – for example, our Brigade has been involved in dealing with firefighter strikes, foot and mouth disease and responding to severe flooding.

There is no such thing as a typical day in the Army Reserve. When we are on camp we may be involved in a variety of activities, including battle simulations, working with other NATO forces from different countries, and repairing and maintaining equipment. The Army Reserve are an essential support to the regular army and we have to make sure we are prepared to be deployed if we are called upon.

I love my job with the Army Reserve – not only is it very different from my day job, but I also get the chance to contribute to the safety and security of our nation, which is a tremendous responsibility. The teamwork and camaraderie of the unit is excellent and I have met people from all walks of life who share the same goals as I do. I'm proud to be a part of the Army Reserve.

Think about it

1 What topics have you covered in this unit so far which might give you the knowledge to understand what an Army Reserve soldier does?

2 What skills and knowledge do you think you need to develop further if you want to be involved in the British Army in the future?

3 How do the Army Reserve and the regular army work together to ensure the defence of the nation?

This section gives you the chance to think more about the role that this person does, and whether you would want to follow in their footsteps once you have completed your BTEC.

37

BTEC Assessment Zone

You will be assessed in two different ways for your BTEC First in Public Services qualification. For most units, your tutor will set assignments for you to complete. These may take the form of projects where you research, plan, prepare, and evaluate a piece of work or activity. The table in this BTEC Assessment Zone explains what you must do in order to achieve each of the assessment criteria. Each unit of this book contains a number of assessment activities to help you with these assessment criteria.

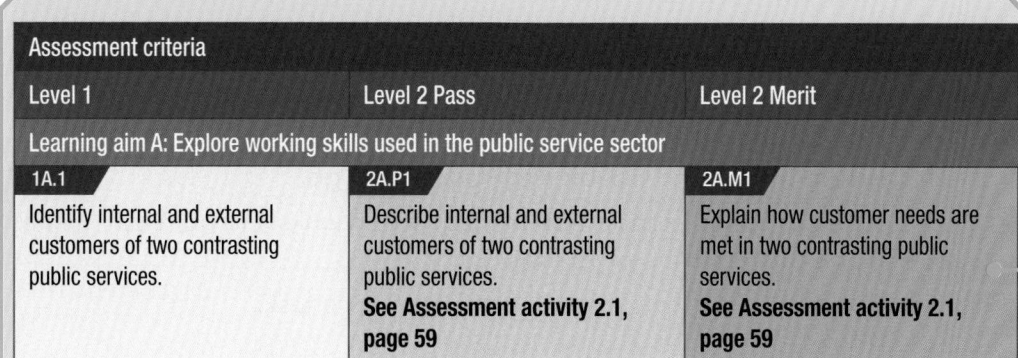

Assessment criteria		
Level 1	Level 2 Pass	Level 2 Merit
Learning aim A: Explore working skills used in the public service sector		
1A.1	2A.P1	2A.M1
Identify internal and external customers of two contrasting public services.	Describe internal and external customers of two contrasting public services. **See Assessment activity 2.1, page 59**	Explain how customer needs are met in two contrasting public services. **See Assessment activity 2.1, page 59**

The table in the BTEC Assessment Zone explains what you must do in order to achieve each of the assessment criteria, and signposts assessment activities in this book to help you to prepare for your assignments.

For Unit 1 of your BTEC, you will be assessed by a paper-based examination. The BTEC Assessment Zone for this unit helps you to prepare for your examination by showing you some of the different types of questions you will need to answer.

A Questions where all of the answers are available and you have to choose the correct answer(s). *Tip: Always read the instructions carefully. Sometimes you may need to identify more than one correct answer.*

Examples:

Public services can be grouped by the type of work they do. Identify the **two** services from the following list that are voluntary. [2]

A   The Police Service

B   Victim Support

C   HM Prison Service

D   The Royal Marines

E   British Red Cross

Answers: B and E

Identify the statement which best describes how the emergency services are funded. [1]

A   Mainly from tax

B   Mainly from donations

C   Mainly from charging for their services

Answer: A

You will find examples of the different types of questions you may need to answer, as well as sample answers and tips on how to prepare for the paper-based examination.

Take it further

If you become distracted by social networking sites or texts when you are working, set yourself a time limit of 10 minutes or so to indulge yourself. You could even use this as a reward for completing a certain amount of work.

▶ Planning and getting organised

The first step in managing your time is to plan ahead and be well organised. Some people are naturally good at this. They think ahead, write down commitments in a diary or planner and store their notes and handouts neatly and carefully so they can find them quickly.

How good are your working habits?

Improving your planning and organisational skills

1 Use a diary to schedule working times into your weekdays and weekends.

2 Also use the diary to write down exactly what work you have to do. You could use this as a 'to do' list and tick off each task as you go.

3 Divide up long or complex tasks into manageable chunks and put each 'chunk' in your diary with a deadline of its own.

4 Always allow more time than you think you need for a task.

▶ Sources of information

You will need to use research to complete your BTEC First assignments, so it is important to know what sources of information are available to you. These are likely to include the following:

Key term

Bias – People often have strong opinions about certain topics. This is called 'bias'. Newspaper or magazine articles, or information found on the internet, may be biased to present a specific point of view.

Textbooks
These cover the units of your qualification and provide activities and ideas for further research.

Internet
A vast source of information, but not all sites are accurate and information and opinions can often be **biased** – you should always double-check facts you find online.

Sources of information

Newspapers and magazines
These often cover public services topics in articles about current affairs or world news.

People
People you know can be a great source of opinions and experience – particularly if you want feedback on an idea.

Television
Programmes such as *Traffic Cops* or *Fighting on the Frontline* can give you an insight into the public services.

Remember!

Store relevant information when you find it – keep a folder on your computer specifically for research – so you do not have to worry about finding it again at a later date.

Organising and selecting information

Organising your information

Once you have used a range of sources of information for research, you will need to organise the information so it is easy to use.

- Make sure your written notes are neat and have a clear heading – it's often useful to date them, too.
- Always keep a note of where the information came from (the title of a book, the title and date of a newspaper or magazine and the web address of a website) and, if relevant, which pages.
- Work out the results of any questionnaires you have used.

Selecting your information

Once you have completed your research, re-read the assignment brief or instructions you were given to remind yourself of the exact wording of the question(s) and divide your information into three groups:

1 Information that is totally relevant.

2 Information that is not as good, but which could come in useful.

3 Information that does not match the questions or assignment brief very much, but that you kept because you could not find anything better!

Check that there are no obvious gaps in your information against the questions or assignment brief. If there are, make a note of them so that you know exactly what you still have to find.

Presenting your work

Before handing in any assignments, make sure:

- you have addressed each part of the question and your work is as complete as possible
- all spelling and grammar is correct
- you have referenced all sources of information you used for your research
- that all work is your own – otherwise you could be committing **plagiarism**
- you have saved a copy of your work.

Key term

Plagiarism – If you are including other people's views, comments or opinions, or copying a diagram or table from another publication, you must state the source by including the name of the author or publication, or the web address. Failure to do this (so you are really pretending other people's work is your own) is known as plagiarism. Check your school's policy on plagiarism and copying.

Introduction

Have you ever thought about how the public services you use are provided, or how many public services you come into contact with every week?

This unit will introduce you to the role and work of the public services. The range and extent of the public services might surprise you. When people think about public services they often think only about uniformed services such as the Police Service or Ambulance Service, but the public services are much broader than this. Many of them do not have a high profile, but without them we could not have the quality of life we enjoy.

This unit will help you to explore what the public services do and how they are funded. You will also learn how funding has an impact on the services and how the public services are held accountable. This unit covers a wide range of organisations and you will also be able to see how they depend on each other to deliver their services.

Assessment: This unit will be assessed externally using a 60-minute paper-based examination.

Learning aims

In this unit you will:

A explore the public services and their work

B understand how public services are delivered.

We did this unit first. It was a really good way of finding out about all of the public services and how they have to rely on each other to be able to do their jobs. I was really surprised by how many public services there are and all the things they do for us that we don't even see.

Priya, *16-year-old Public Services student*

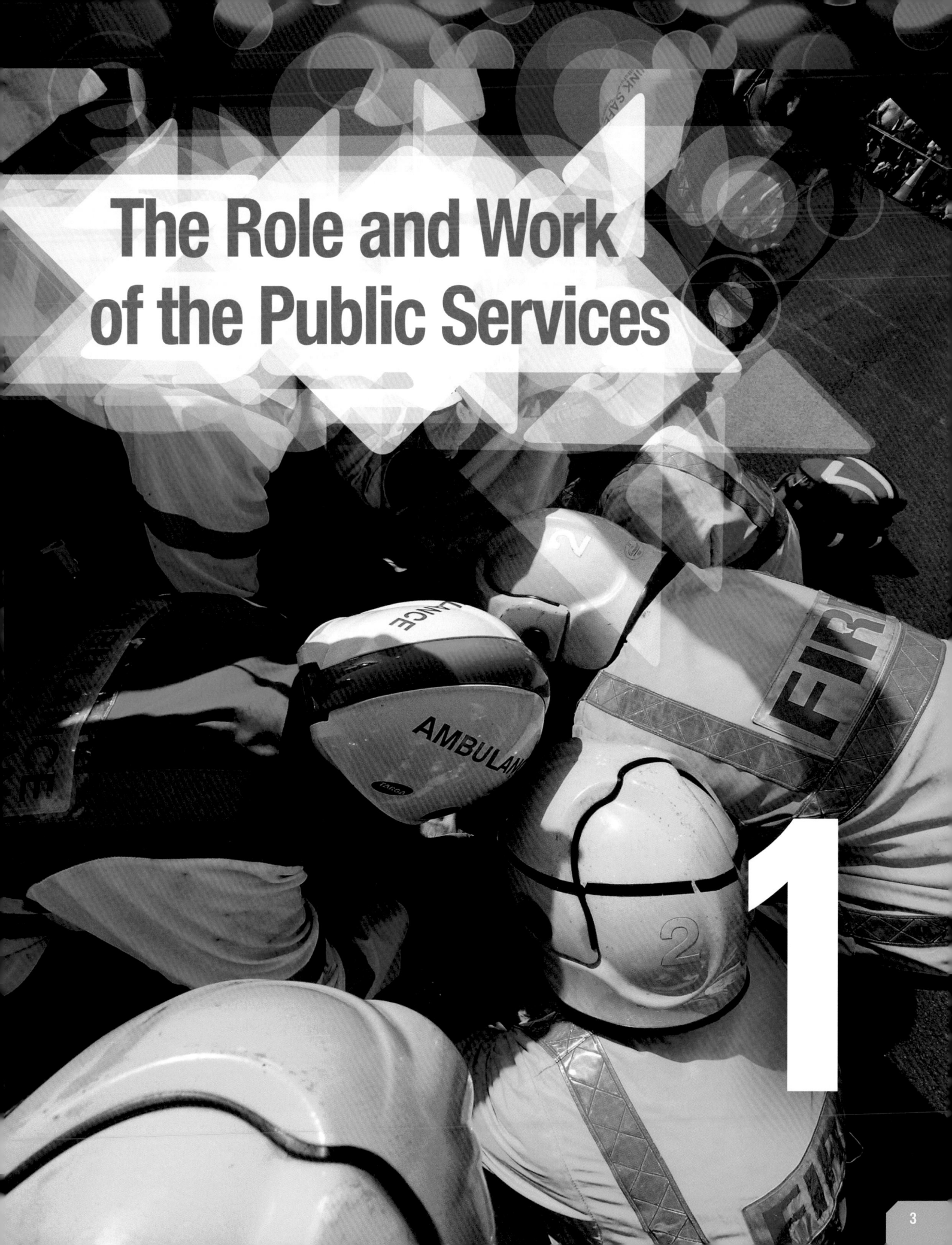

The Role and Work of the Public Services

1

▶ Grouping and purpose of the public services

Introduction

It is useful to know how the public service sector is structured, the types of public service in the sector and the services they provide. There are probably more services than you think and they carry out a wider range of jobs than you imagine. Think about how many public services you can name and list some examples of the jobs they might do.

One thing all the services have in common is that they exist to serve the public. The public services fall into five broad groups:

- emergency services
- armed services
- central government
- local authorities
- voluntary services.

It is important to remember that these different groups of services work together very closely and, although grouping them up is helpful when you are learning about what they do, each service can fall into more than one category. For example:

- the Mountain Rescue service is a 999 service in some areas of the country, but it is also a voluntary service and relies on charitable donations to fund its work
- the Prison Service may not be classified as an emergency service, but it can be called upon to respond to emergency situations in prisons, such as riots
- the British Army can be called upon to assist other public services when a major incident occurs, such as widespread flooding or a terrorist attack.

▶ The emergency services

The emergency services are sometimes called the 'blue light' services, because of the flashing lights on their vehicles. They respond to civilian emergencies reported via 999 calls. These services are usually the Police Service, the Fire and Rescue Service and the Ambulance Service. Emergency services may also include HM Coastguard and Mountain Rescue.

They have a responsibility to respond quickly and effectively in cases of **incident**, accident or emergency and to prevent incidents where possible.

The Police Service

The modern Police Service in England and Wales was formed in 1829 by the Home Secretary, Sir Robert Peel, who created the Metropolitan Police Act. Police services in counties outside of the London metropolitan area were created by the County Police Act 1839.

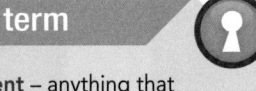
Key term

Incident – anything that requires attention by the public services. It could be a fire, a serious motorway crash or a fight outside a pub.

Case study

In December 2013, the east coast of England suffered severe flooding after the worst storm surge in 60 years. Areas such as Lincolnshire, Norfolk and East Yorkshire were particularly affected, with towns such as Boston extensively flooded. Emergency services from across the affected areas responded to the flooding with rescue and evacuation activity, and local authorities set up alternative accommodation in public buildings such as local schools and leisure centres. The emergency services were supported by the British Army. Support included:

- 95 soldiers from the Second Battalion of the Parachute Regiment (2 PARA) assisted with the evacuation of homes in Southend and Maldon
- 60 soldiers from the Light Dragoons built flood defences at an electrical sub-station in Great Yarmouth
- the provision of Prince William of Gloucester Barracks in Grantham as an evacuation rest centre, which received approximately 100 civilian evacuees.

Working together is essential for all the services regardless of which group they belong to.

1 Why is it necessary for the services to work together in a flooding situation such as the one described?

2 What types of things can the army do to support the emergency services?

3 Why would the emergency services call upon the army for support?

4 How does responding to emergencies benefit the army?

Discussion

The Police Service as we currently know it is still less than 200 years old.

Working in small groups, discuss the following questions.

- Why do you think we needed to create a new Police Service in 1829?
- What are the advantages and disadvantages of having a Police Service?
- Could we manage without a Police Service in today's society?

Did you know?

Police officers are sometimes referred to as 'bobbies' after the founder of the Police Service, Sir Robert Peel.

The police do a great deal more work than we may realise. As well as responding to emergency calls and investigating crime, their responsibilities include:

- improving community relations
- reducing the fear of crime by maintaining a visible presence on the streets
- working in partnership with other services to reduce and prevent crime
- giving evidence in court
- educational visits to schools/colleges
- licensing firearms
- referring victims of crime to support agencies
- conducting underwater searches
- filing missing persons reports
- providing advice and information on personal safety and protection of property
- escorting abnormal loads
- holding people in police custody
- dealing with public protests or public order incidents
- managing and responding to major incidents.

The Fire and Rescue Service

Private firefighting companies were the main formal response to fire until the 1800s, when government began to take over responsibility for firefighting. The 1938 Fire Brigades Act required local authorities to ensure that their area had an effective fire service. The main piece of current legislation that outlines what the fire service does is the Fire and Rescue Services Act 2004.

Today there are 46 separate fire authorities in England, employing around 27,000 full-time firefighters and around 11,000 retained (part-time) firefighters.

How has the Fire and Rescue Service evolved over time?

Apart from responding to emergency calls in the case of fire or serious road traffic incidents, the Fire and Rescue Service is also required to:

- promote fire safety
- ensure fire prevention
- respond to road, rail and air traffic accidents
- give first aid at scenes of accidents
- manage disasters and respond to floods
- handle incidents involving hazardous materials
- give evidence in court
- preserve evidence at the scene of a deliberate fire (arson)
- offer fire safety advice in the home
- deal with terrorist incidents if required.

The Ambulance Service

The modern Ambulance Service is largely linked with the development of the National Health Service (NHS), and so it dates from about 1946. When you think of the Ambulance Service, at first you may think of paramedics, but there is a whole range of roles in the service, such as:

- patient transport
- emergency care assistants
- medical dispatchers
- emergency call handlers.

They all have to work together to ensure a prompt response to emergency situations.

The Ambulance Service has the primary objectives of responding to life-threatening emergencies, delivering emergency care and supplying transportation to hospital, but there are other aspects of their role you may not be familiar with, including:

- non-emergency patient transport
- transfers of patients between hospitals
- delivery of first aid courses
- clinical staffing for air ambulances
- decontamination of casualties.

Discussion

If you needed to call 999 for assistance do you know what information you would need to give? Conduct some research and make a list of all the things the operator would ask you about the incident.

Did you know?

Ambulance crews must reach 75% of life-threatening calls within 8 minutes. 95% of life threatening calls must receive an ambulance within 19 minutes.

Activity 1.1	Emergency services working together

There are many occasions when the emergency services must work together in order to protect life and property.

1 List their key responsibilities at the scene of a major incident and identify how they must work together to achieve their aims.

2 List the possible consequences if they do not work together effectively.

The armed services

The armed services respond to external threats made either to our nation directly or to our civilians and financial interests abroad. They are collectively responsible for the defence of our nation and its resources. They include:

- the British Army
- the Royal Navy
- the Royal Air Force (RAF).

These primary services are supported by the reserve forces:

- the Army Reserve (formerly known as the Territorial Army)
- the Royal Naval Reserve
- the RAF Reserves.

The armed services in the UK have around 170,000 trained personnel. They also employ around 65,000 civilian support workers. They have three key priorities.

1 **Defending the UK** – the armed services work together to protect the UK from attack by external sources. The forces are also required to work with our allies to defend other countries, both in Europe and worldwide. This is because we are members of NATO (the North Atlantic Treaty Organization). Defending the UK includes defending its overseas interests, such as territory overseas. The armed services also assist with the evacuation of British nationals in countries experiencing conflict. For example, in December 2013, the RAF sent a C-17 Globemaster III aircraft to rescue British, European Union and Commonwealth citizens who were fleeing conflict in South Sudan.

Did you know?

Some people think of the Royal Marines as a separate armed service, but they are actually part of the Royal Navy.

Why is it important that the UK armed services work effectively together?

2 **Supporting international peacekeeping duties** – the armed services work with international organisations such as NATO and the United Nations (UN) to protect civilians and aid workers in some of the most dangerous parts of the world. In January 2014, the UK had 280 troops on peacekeeping mission in Cyprus with the UN and around 5,000 troops deployed to the UN's International Security Assistance Force (ISAF) in Afghanistan. The majority of British troops are located in Helmand Province in southern Afghanistan. Over 400 UK troops have been killed in Afghanistan since ISAF was created in 2001.

3 **Supporting the civil authorities** – the armed services are sometimes called upon to assist their emergency service and local authority counterparts in times of disaster, unrest or emergency. This has happened in recent years in the case of flood defence and rescue, and also in the case of public service strikes. For example, during the national fire strike in 2002, the armed services covered firefighting duties.

Did you know?

During the 1982 Falklands War, the British Overseas Territory of the Falkland Islands was invaded by Argentine forces. The resulting conflict lasted 74 days before the Argentinians surrendered; 256 British and approximately 750 Argentinian service personnel were killed in the conflict.

Discussion

NATO is a group of 28 countries across Europe and North America who work together to defend each other, promote democracy and reduce international conflict. The organisation was set up after the Second World War, and an attack on one member is seen as an attack on all members.

In small groups, discuss the following questions.

* Why might an organisation such as NATO have been created after the Second World War?
* What are the advantages and disadvantages of being part of a group such as NATO?

The British Army

The British Army is one of the few modern armies to be based on the **regimental system**, which means that a soldier or an officer will normally serve in the same regiment throughout their career. Each regiment has its own history and traditions, and this system encourages loyalty to a regiment, which boosts troops' fighting spirit and motivation. The British Army employs over 80,000 servicemen and women.

The Royal Navy

Because Britain is an island, the defence of our coast has always been very important. The Royal Navy protects Britain from invaders and also protects our trade routes to Europe and the rest of the world.

The first permanent navy was established in 1546 by Henry VIII and it has played a major role in every significant conflict since, either supporting ground troops or engaging in active combat. Today, the Royal Navy employs over 30,000 servicemen and women who can be deployed on ships, submarines and naval bases around the world.

Key term

Regimental system – a way of organising a fighting force so that each soldier is recruited, trained and administered by the regiment in which they serve for their entire career. It creates intense loyalty to the regiment.

Did you know? ?

The original uniform of the Royal Naval Reserves distinguished them from their regular counterparts by its wavy gold lace. This led to them being called the 'Wavy Navy'.

The Royal Air Force (RAF)

The RAF was created by an Act of Parliament in 1917. As well as direct combat, the RAF's early missions focused on gathering aerial intelligence on enemy troop positions and armaments, which helped British troops gain a tactical advantage. The RAF now employs around 35,000 servicemen and women in a variety of roles, including pilot, ground support, mechanic and air traffic controller.

Reserve forces

Each service has a reserve force, which can be called up to serve during times of conflict or crisis. These forces are made up of civilians who have other day jobs and train as soldiers, sailors or pilots in their spare time (see Table 1.1).

Table 1.1: British reserve forces.

Reserve force	Description
Army Reserve (formerly known as the Territorial Army or TA)	• Largest of the reserve forces. • Provides support to regular troops serving overseas. • Made up of two groups: ▪ regular reservists who were once full-time soldiers but have left the service ▪ Army Reserve soldiers who work part-time as soldiers while doing other jobs in other professions. • The government plans to shrink the size of the regular army to 82,000 by 2020 and increase the size of the reserves to 30,000.
Royal Naval Reserve (RNR)	• Provides part-time trained support to the Royal Navy. • Comprises 2,300 men and women who can be deployed with the Royal Navy in times of conflict. • Current reservists have served with regular forces all around the world.
RAF Reserves (Royal Auxiliary Air Force)	• Deployed to support their regular counterparts in times of conflict. • Comprises 24 squadrons based across the country.

Assessment practice 1.1

1 Identify two armed service reserves. [2]

2 Identify the three main functions of the armed services. [3]

3 Explain how the armed service reserves work with their regular counterparts. [2]

Local authorities

Local authorities work to deliver local services such as education, refuse collection and recycling, social care, street lighting and road repair. Each type of local authority has different responsibilities, which are shown in Table 1.2.

Table 1.2: Different types of local authority.

Type	Description
County councils	• Responsible for services across the whole of a county, such as planning, transport, libraries, social care, waste management, trading standards, public safety, education.
District, borough and city councils	• Cover areas smaller than counties. • Often responsible for services such as council tax collection, recycling, refuse collection and recycling, and housing. • Report to the county council.
Unitary authorities	• Large local authorities which carry out all the duties of both county and district councils.
Parish and town councils	• Parts of local government that work below the level of district councils. • Responsible for services such as community centres, allotments, bus shelters, play areas, litter, graffiti and neighbourhood planning.

Local authorities provide many different services to the people who live in their area. Some of these services are shown in Figure 1.1.

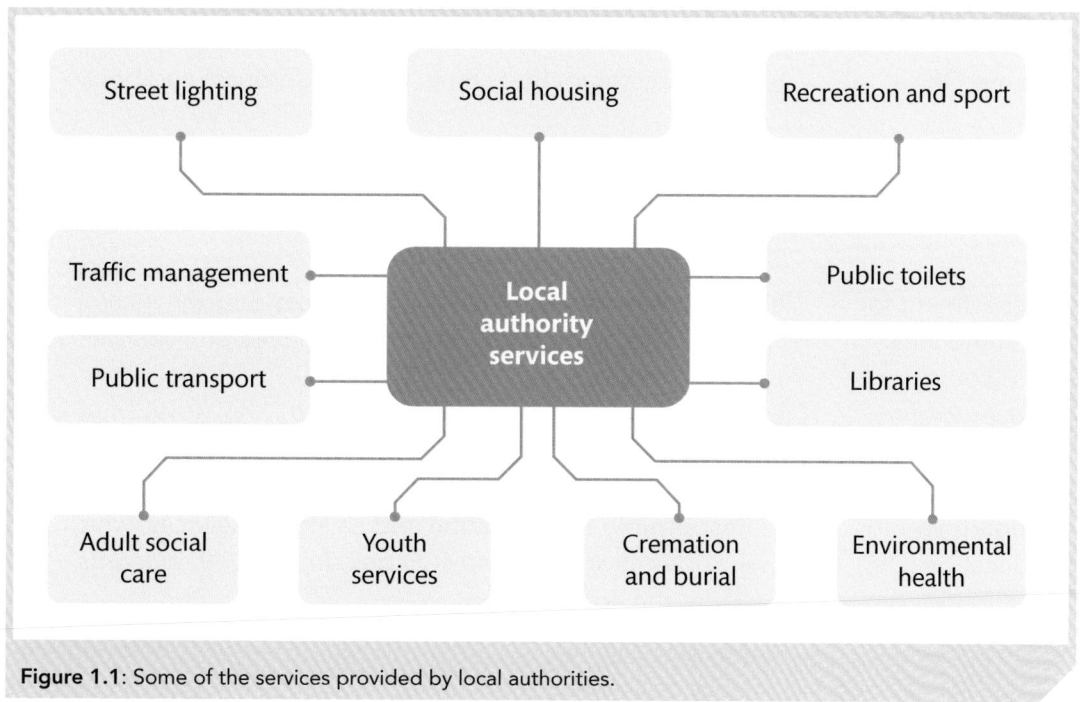

Figure 1.1: Some of the services provided by local authorities.

Over 1.5 million people are employed in local government nationally so it is a very big part of public sector employment opportunities. There are over 350 local authorities in England and Wales.

Local areas have different requirements, so central government would find it difficult to operate services nationally. Services are best delivered locally by people who know and understand the local area.

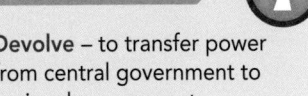

Key term

Devolve – to transfer power from central government to regional government.

▶ Central government

Central government is the top level of government. In the UK, central government is based at Westminster in the Houses of Parliament. In addition, Scotland, Wales and Northern Ireland also have **devolved** national parliaments.

Central government is made up of 650 Members of Parliament (MPs). Each one represents a geographical region of the UK called a constituency.

Central government also has a number of departments or 'ministries' that undertake specific jobs and run the public services of the country. There are 24 ministries in total (such as the Department of Transport and the Department for Business, Innovation and Skills) and central government is responsible for each one and the agencies that report to them. Each government department has a minister in charge who reports to the Prime Minister on the work of that department. The ministries in Table 1.3 are directly related to armed, emergency, non-emergency and voluntary sector public services.

Table 1.3: Ministries relating to public services.

Ministry	Description
Ministry of Defence (MOD)	<ul><li>Responsible for the security of the UK.</li><li>Responsible for all three armed services and their reserves.</li><li>Employs approximately 65,000 civilian personnel and nearly 170,000 members of the armed services.</li></ul>
Home Office	<ul><li>Leads on combating crime, counterterrorism and border control.</li><li>Responsible for public services such as the Police Service, the Security Service (MI5), UK Visas and Immigration and Border Force.</li></ul>
Department for Communities and Local Government	<ul><li>Responsible for the delivery of services through local councils, including refuse collection, children's services and social housing.</li><li>Also responsible for the 46 Fire and Rescue Authorities, so the Fire and Rescue Service sits within this department.</li></ul>
Department for Education (DfE)	<ul><li>Responsible for education and children's services, which includes all schools and colleges dealing with students under the age of 19.</li></ul>

continued

Table 1.3 continued

Ministry	Description
Department of Health	• Responsible for GP surgeries, hospitals, disease control and prevention, and the Ambulance Service. • Acts to ensure we can all live better, longer lives.
Foreign and Commonwealth Office	• Responsible for intelligence services such as the Secret Intelligence Service (SIS or MI6) and Government Communications Headquarters (GCHQ). • Supports British overseas interests as well as British citizens living, working or holidaying abroad. • Works to combat overseas terrorism and reduce international conflict. • Works closely with the Ministry of Defence when the UK is involved in overseas conflict.
Ministry of Justice (MoJ)	• Responsible for the courts, Prison Service and National Probation Service (NPS). • Works to reduce criminal behaviour and reoffending.

Activity 1.2   Services and government departments

Look at the eight services below and match each one to the government department that is responsible for it.

Public service	Government department
Police Service	Ministry of Justice
Prison Service	Foreign and Commonwealth Office
MI6	Department for Communities and Local Government
Fire and Rescue Service	Department for Education
RAF	Department of Health
Primary schools	Home Office
Ambulance Service	Ministry of Defence

1 The probation service is part of the Ministry of Justice. Identify one
other service that is managed by the Ministry of Justice. [1]

2 Explain the term 'incident' in a public service context. [1]

3 List six services provided by local authorities. [6]

Voluntary or third sector services

Voluntary services are sometimes called the third sector because they pick up work
that is not done by the public or private sector. Voluntary services usually support the
following three services:

- the emergency services (see Table 1.4)
- the social services (see Table 1.5)
- the health services (see Table 1.6).

The government has limited money and so cannot do everything it would like.
Volunteer services step in to fill this gap and enable support to be given to individuals
and families in need who might not receive help otherwise. They rely largely on public
donations and the work of unpaid volunteers.

Table 1.4: Volunteer services supporting the emergency services.

Service	Description
Royal National Lifeboat Institution (RNLI)	• Provides 24-hour search and rescue services and beach lifeguard services. • Has saved more than 140,000 lives since it was founded in 1824. • Rescues on average 23 people every day.
Mountain and Cave Rescue services	• Operate in mountainous parts of the country, rescuing lost or injured people. • Operate in areas with large cave networks, such as Derbyshire and the Yorkshire Dales. • Made up of people who may live locally and know the terrain very well, as well as having expertise in mountain weather conditions and cave rescue techniques.
Royal Voluntary Service (RVS)	• Helps older people stay active and engaged with their local community. • One of the largest volunteer organisations in the UK with over 40,000 volunteers.

continued

Table 1.4 continued

Service	Description
The British Red Cross	• Humanitarian organisation that helps people in crisis. • Originally established in 1870 as a neutral source of help to sick and wounded soldiers. • Provides support such as first aid training, emergency response, disaster preparation and refugee support.
St John Ambulance	• Provides first aid training to individuals who may then go on to be volunteers, acting either as backup for the Ambulance Service as first responders or providing first aid at public events. • Has over 40,000 adult and junior members.

Table 1.5: Volunteer services supporting the social services.

Service	Description
National Society for the Prevention of Cruelty to Children (NSPCC)	• Works to end neglect and abuse of children. • Founded in 1884. • Employs over 2,000 people across the UK. • Around 90% of the NSPCC's income is donated by the public.
Shelter	• Works to provide good-quality affordable housing and to combat homelessness. • Founded in 1966. • Employs more than 1,000 people nationally. • Over 50% of its income is donated by members of the public and businesses.
Women's Aid	• Works to end violence against women and children, and campaigns on issues such as domestic and sexual violence. • Established in 1974. • Employs around 35 paid staff. The rest of the staff base is made up of volunteers.
Samaritans	• Supports individuals who feel depressed or suicidal. • Runs a 24-hour helpline, which receives a call every six seconds. • Has over 20,000 volunteers across the UK. • 80% of its income comes from charitable donations.

 Did you know?

The number of people who need help puts strain on the public services. For example, available data suggests that 31% of women and 18% of men have experienced domestic abuse since the age of 16. The public services alone could not deal with such huge numbers of victims. This is why organisations such as Women's Aid and the Men's Advice Line are a vital source of support for the public services.

Take it further

- Consider the range of voluntary services that offer support to the public sector. Research three of them in detail and produce a leaflet that describes how they help a specific public service.
- Joining the public services is a very competitive business. Could you work with any of these charities to improve your skills and get to know more about your community and yourself?

Table 1.6: Volunteer services supporting the health services.

Service	Description
British Heart Foundation	• Funds and conducts heart research in the UK. • Campaigns to raise awareness of the health of the heart.
Mind	• Supports people who suffer from mental health issues. • Campaigns for better research into, and treatment of, mental health disorders. • Campaigns to reduce prejudice against those experiencing mental health problems.
Cancer Research UK	• Funds research into the prevention, causes and treatments of cancer.

Assessment practice 1.3

1 Explain how the voluntary services support the public services. [2]
2 Explain why the voluntary sector is sometimes called the third sector. [1]

TOPIC A.2

▶ The work and responsibilities of the public services

Introduction

Although the public services work closely together, and often in similar situations, the jobs they do are actually quite different. In this topic, you will look at the purpose, role and responsibilities of a variety of public services. Think of a public service you know and consider the range of tasks it is responsible for.

Key term

Statutory – required by law. A statute is another name for a law or Act of Parliament.

▶ Statutory responsibilities

Public services often have **statutory** responsibilities. These are tasks they must carry out by law, not by choice. If budgets are tight, statutory roles and responsibilities will take priority over other responsibilities.

For example, the Fire and Rescue Service has a number of statutory duties, such as:

- promoting fire safety
- emergency response and rescue
- fire, petroleum and explosives regulatory enforcement.

Non-statutory services

Non-statutory services are services provided by public services or charities that are not formally required by law. They are delivered by choice and usually accompany statutory services. For example, the NHS provides a whole range of non-statutory services, including:

- walk-in centres
- dental access centres
- health promotion units.

They are provided in addition to the statutory services of the NHS and **complement** those services.

Other non-statutory services include charitable public services such as Victim Support and the Royal National Lifeboat Institution.

Contracted-out services

When public services contract out services (either statutory or non-statutory services), this means that they hand the operational delivery of a particular service to a private or voluntary provider. This is sometimes called **outsourcing**.

Local authorities deliver a lot of their services by contracting them out, as it is seen to be a more cost-effective way of delivering the service. It has been estimated that over £80 billion of local authority services are outsourced to private companies and the voluntary sector. The advantages and disadvantages of contracting out are outlined in Table 1.7.

Services that are commonly contracted out include:

- refuse collection and waste management
- Meals on Wheels
- adult social care
- social housing repair and maintenance
- ICT support
- highway maintenance.

Table 1.7: The advantages and disadvantages of contracting out.

Advantages	Disadvantages
Can be cost effective.	Can lead to fraud and corruption in the awarding of contracts.
Can improve efficiency.	May meet resistance from unions who feel that contracting out services erodes workers' terms and conditions.

continued

Discussion

- Local authorities face a challenge. They must continue to provide statutory services while making budget cuts of around 28%. These cuts will take place between 2011 and 2015, with planned decreases beyond 2015.
- How do you think local authorities can continue to deliver such a vast range of statutory services with less funding?

Key terms

Complement – add to something (such as a service) in a way which enhances it.

Outsourcing – when a public service contracts a private company to provide a service on its behalf.

Take it further

There is a new idea called 'in-sourcing' which means moving services back under local authority direct delivery. Conduct some research on in-sourcing – can you find any examples of a local authority moving services back in-house?

Table 1.7 continued

Advantages	Disadvantages
Can create increased flexibility.	Work can be of inferior quality.
Can reduce management and administrative burdens.	The focus is on profit rather than the quality of the service.
Can reduce the need for capital investment in equipment.	The lowest bid usually wins, regardless of quality.
Can provide access to expert skills and innovative ways of working.	Can increase costs if not carefully monitored.

The work and purpose of public services

When you think of the public services you are likely to think first of services in uniform, such as the emergency or armed services. However, there are many other public services which are less well known that provide key services and employment opportunities. Some of these opportunities are found within central government, local authorities and the voluntary sector.

Education and training services

Education has been around for as long as there have been people who needed to learn new skills and abilities. Education does not just mean learning in schools and colleges – it also means learning from any source, such as books, the internet, parents and grandparents, or employers.

In the past, the vast majority of people in the UK had no formal education at all. Today's society is very different. We rely on our technological and academic skills to compete economically with other countries, so our schools, colleges and universities have to provide us with the skills and knowledge to do so. In modern Britain, people of all ages and from all sections of society can receive education.

The responsibility for education in the UK is shared between two government departments.

- **The Department for Education** – responsible for the education of young people from the ages of 5 to 18. This includes primary, junior and secondary schools, as well as provision for 14- to 18-year-olds in further education (FE) colleges.
- **The Department for Business, Innovation and Skills** – responsible for the education of adults and apprentices. This includes further education (FE) colleges, universities, and private training providers (PTPs).

The National Health Service (NHS)

The NHS was created by the National Health Service Act 1946. Before this, people had to pay for medical treatment, which disadvantaged poorer people who could not afford treatment. The NHS operates on the principle of being free at the point of use, which means that British citizens can access healthcare without paying directly for treatment.

The NHS operates key health services such as:

- hospitals
- clinics
- GP surgeries
- dental surgeries
- optical services.

The NHS employs more than 1.7 million people, including:

- around 370,000 nurses
- around 105,000 medically-trained hospital and dental staff
- around 39,000 GPs
- around 18,000 ambulance staff.

These roles are supported by managers and administrators who help the service to run smoothly. The annual budget of the NHS in 2012/13 was over £108 billion. It is managed by the Department of Health.

Public health services

Public health services are designed to help people to stay healthy and educate them to make sensible and informed choices about their health in order to minimise the risk of illness. The services provided include:

- sexual health clinics
- alcohol services
- drugs education
- advice on stopping smoking.

Public health services are also concerned with educating people to help them make sensible and informed choices about their health in order to minimise the risk of illness. They draw attention to key issues by running public health campaigns, such as:

- Change4Life
- Stoptober
- cancer awareness campaigns.

Did you know?

The NHS deals with over 1 million patients every 36 hours.

Did you know?

The NHS is the fourth largest employer in the world. The Chinese People's Liberation Army, the American supermarket chain Walmart and the Indian Railways are the only organisations to directly employ more people than the NHS.

Activity 1.3 / Rising health costs

Consider the following information.

- Smoking-related illness costs the NHS more than £5 billion per year, with around 18% of deaths each year attributed to smoking.
- In 2012, a survey found that 26% of adults in the UK were obese. Diseases caused by poor diet and sedentary lifestyles cost the NHS more than £6 billion a year.
- There are around 1 million admissions to hospital each year as a result of alcohol, costing an estimated £2.7 billion every year.
- With good public health campaigns, the NHS could save approximately £12.7 billion each year on preventable lifestyle-related health problems such as those listed above.

Design a public health campaign on obesity, alcohol or smoking to educate people about how to keep themselves healthy, highlighting the savings that could be made.

Defence

The defence of our nation is overseen by the Ministry of Defence (MOD). It controls all three armed services to defend our national interests (see pages 8–10).

The Home Office

The Home Office has a range of responsibilities including the Police Service (see pages 4–6). It is also responsible for our borders and immigration. This includes:

- **UK Visas and Immigration** – deals with visa applications and applications for asylum
- **Border Force** – checks travellers' immigration statuses and searches for illegal goods or immigrants.

Her Majesty's Treasury (HM Treasury)

HM Treasury is the government's finance department. It works to keep the economy on track and manages public spending. It sets the budgets for other government departments, so it is very important to the public services.

It is also the government department responsible for collecting tax, so it has responsibility for Her Majesty's Revenue and Customs (HMRC). HMRC is a public service with the following priorities:

- tax collection
- **excise duties**
- National Insurance
- tax credits
- child benefit
- enforcement of the national minimum wage.

HMRC also ensures that goods coming in and out of the country are legitimate and have had tax paid on them. It employs around 66,000 staff, including the customs officers at ports and airports.

Social services

Social services provide social care for vulnerable adults and children, as well as family support and support to carers. They provide services such as residential care, child protection services, fostering and adoption.

They are influenced by a variety of central government departments, as shown in Figure 1.2.

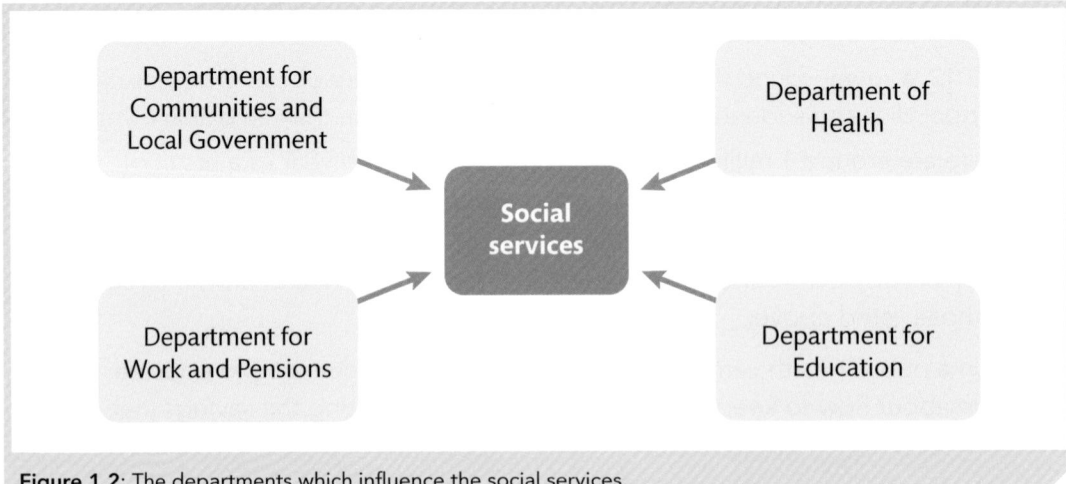

Figure 1.2: The departments which influence the social services.

Did you know?

The UK is home to less than 2% of the world's refugees. 80% of the world's refugees live in the developing world.

Key term

Excise duty – a tax on the sale of goods within a country.

Did you know?

HMRC is a law enforcement agency which investigates serious organised financial crimes, including smuggling and tax evasion.

As with all public services, social services can only do as much as their staffing and budgets allow, and cannot meet the needs of every vulnerable person in society. They often take a great deal of criticism for this, with high-profile failures dominating the media. However, you are less likely to hear about the thousands of people helped by social services whose lives might have been very different if they had not been helped.

Case study

Peter Connelly (referred to as baby P during the court proceedings into his death) was found dead in his cot on 3 August 2007. A post-mortem found that Peter had suffered a catalogue of non-accidental serious injuries and identified his death was not accidental.

Further investigation highlighted a series of interventions made by social services and health departments from the time Peter was nine months old until his death aged 17 months. These included:

- GP spotting bruises on his chest and face
- admission to hospital with bruises, two black eyes and swelling on the side of his head
- marks spotted on his face by a social worker.

Several of these incidents led to the arrest of Peter's mother, but none of the interventions prevented his death. Peter's mother, her boyfriend and her brother were all jailed for Peter's death.

An inquiry was called, examining the role of the police, social services and health services in the case, to find out how multiple opportunities to save Peter from abuse were missed. The family had been visited 60 times by the authorities in the eight months before Peter's death.

1 What are the challenges in getting the police, social services and health services to share information in cases such as this?

2 How can social services tread the line between supporting families and protecting children?

3 Why do you think the failures of social services attract huge media attention, but their successes do not?

4 Social services sometimes have to intervene in awful circumstances. Is this a service you feel you could join? Explain your answer.

Leisure and heritage services

Leisure and heritage services are provided by local authorities and charitable organisations such as English Heritage and the National Trust. These services include sports facilities, libraries, theatres, museums and art galleries. They also include cultural activities such as Bonfire Night, New Year's Eve celebrations and Eid Mela.

Cultural and leisure facilities can be deemed less essential than other services by local authorities. When budgets are tight, this can lead to the closure of facilities such as sports centres and libraries.

Community protection

Community protection is about making the community a safer place in which to live and work. It involves different services, such as the police, environmental health and the local authority, working together to reduce crime, environmental disasters, accidents and incidents. The services involved in community protection also include voluntary services, such as the British Red Cross and St John Ambulance (see pages 14–16 for more information).

Key terms

Prosecute – to carry out legal proceedings against someone.

Try – to put someone on trial.

Custody – in the justice system, this means imprisonment.

Probation – this is the period of time after an offender is released, when they are supervised and must show good behaviour.

Justice

The justice system deals with civil and criminal issues.

- **Civil issues** – one individual takes another individual to court in order to gain compensation for a civil matter, such as a company suing a customer for failing to pay their bill.
- **Criminal issues** – the state or government takes an individual to court for a breach of criminal law and seeks punishment for the crime (for example, someone being prosecuted for murder).

The justice system is made up of several different services. These include:

- the Police Service, which investigates criminal cases
- the Crown Prosecution Service (CPS), which **prosecutes** criminal cases
- courts, which **try** civil and criminal cases
- lawyers, who represent the people who are accused of crimes or the victims of alleged crimes
- Her Majesty's (HM) Prison Service, which keeps people sentenced to prison in **custody**
- the National Offender Management Service (NOMS), which enforces the decisions of the court and ensures that people serve their sentences. NOMS includes the National **Probation** Service.

The Royal Courts of Justice. Which public services make up the justice system?

Environmental protection

Environmental protection is provided by the Department for Environment, Food and Rural Affairs (Defra). Defra works to reduce pollution and waste, and responds to emergencies such as floods. It is supported by local authorities which operate local waste management and environmental health departments. It is important to protect the environment, as pollution and waste can have a negative effect on people's health and life expectancy.

▶ The need for the public services to work together

Introduction

The jobs the public services have to do can be enormous and span the entire country. The public services cannot do all of their tasks on their own – they need to rely on each other to meet their objectives. Can you think of two services which often have to work together? What would happen if they did not work together properly?

▷ Efficiency and sharing information

One reason why public services should work together is because they need to be as efficient as possible and deliver the best possible value for money. They can save money by planning and coordinating their activities together, and by sharing the expertise of their teams. This is especially important when the government has to make savings, some of which come from public service budgets.

Another reason why public services should work together is because the work of different public services often overlaps, particularly in areas such as public health and safety. It is important that the services coordinate their activities to protect the public and businesses.

Some of the reasons why the public services should work together as a team are outlined below.

- **Ensuring continuity of business and day-to-day activities** – the services have a responsibility to ensure that people and businesses can go about their day-to-day activities. Regardless of the incident or situation, everyday life carries on. People will still need to get to work, businesses will need to open and public transport will need to run.

- **Effective utilisation of resources** – public services should share information so they can use their resources effectively. For example, it would be a waste of resources to have both an ambulance crew and St John Ambulance staff at a single event. Instead, one team could staff the event and the other team could be deployed elsewhere.

- **Meeting objectives** – each public service sets its own objectives and also has objectives set for it by government. Working together can help the services to meet their objectives more effectively than by working alone.

- **Public health and safety** – the services need to share information to ensure the public are kept safe at large events, such as New Year's Eve celebrations or sports events.

- **Prevention of crime and terrorism** – preventing crime and terrorism is the responsibility of all public services, but they can only do this effectively if they share information. For example, if a child is abused and an ambulance is called, the medical services must inform the police. If the services did not work together like this, many criminals would not be caught and sentenced.

▶ Working together to manage incidents

An incident is something which requires a response from the public services. These can be large or small, ranging from road traffic incidents and flooding to riots and public disturbances. It is rare for only one public service to have to respond to such incidents. Usually, many services work together to complete the tasks required, as outlined in Table 1.8.

Table 1.8: Managing incidents.

Action	Description
Assess the situation	The services work together to assess the situation and establish which tasks need to be done by which service. The services practise working together regularly so that they know how their roles fit together.
Coordinate rescues	Some services have a very specific role in rescues, such as HM Coastguard, the Royal Navy's Search and Rescue team and Mountain Rescue. These services will usually be supported by other services in coordinating rescues.
Provide emergency medical care	Incidents often involve casualties who need treatment. The services must treat casualties at the scene until they can receive specialist treatment in hospital.
Maintain the security of the incident scene	Some incident scenes are also crime scenes. The services must not allow people to access the area, in order to protect any evidence.
Keep the public away from the scene to ensure the rescue is not impeded	The services must prevent people from gathering round the scene of an incident because this can prevent the public services from dealing with the incident. It can even put members of the public in danger. The police deploy cordons to keep the public away, using barricade tape, cars and patrols.
Minimise the impact of incidents on the wider community	Serious crime can have a lasting impact on the wider community, leading to an increased fear of crime or the closure of homes and businesses. To reassure the public, the services may maintain a visible presence in the area for a while after an incident.

Communication pathways

Effective communication is key to the public services working together effectively. Some of the key aspects are outlined below.

- **Orders and instructions are passed down quickly and accurately** – if orders are delayed, the actions of the services will be held up, and this could cost lives and property. If orders are not given accurately, the wrong action could be taken, which could have serious consequences.

- **Leaders are kept informed of developments** – senior officers in the public services are often the ones who make strategic decisions. However, sometimes they are not at the front line of an incident, so they have to rely on reports from officers at the scene to know what is going on. These reports have to be frequent and accurate if senior officers are going to be able to make decisions and support their front line staff.

- **Communication systems such as radios are compatible** – public services must be able to speak with each other while dealing with an incident. This means that their radios must be compatible, and there can be serious consequences if they are not (see case study).

- **Information is passed to people not at the scene who have an interest** – the public services need to ensure that people such as relatives of victims and the media have access to information about the incident. In some circumstances, it is in the interests of the public services to issue guidance and warnings to as many people as possible. For example, flood alerts can be relayed quickly using local radio and television.

Case study

In 1987, 31 people died in a fire at the King's Cross Underground Station in London. The inquiry into the incident raised serious concerns about the compatibility of communications between London Underground staff and the emergency services. As a result, a series of recommendations were made which were designed to ensure that all emergency services and London Underground staff were able to communicate in the event of a serious incident.

On 7 July 2005, the London Underground suffered a terrorist attack which killed 52 people. At the time of the incident, London Underground communications were still not compatible with those of the emergency services, despite the recommendations of the King's Cross inquiry 18 years earlier.

This meant that during the emergency response to the 7/7 bombings, rescuers were unable to request additional support or relay information effectively to the surface, which hampered rescue efforts.

1 Why is it important that transport systems like the London Underground are able to communicate with the emergency services during an incident?

2 What are the possible consequences of a communication failure?

3 What might prevent the services from making their different communication systems compatible with each other? Can you think of any difficulties?

Did you know?

The emergency services use a radio system called Airwave. This is a secure and encrypted system which provides inter-operability between the public services.

Like the emergency services, the armed services also need to be able to communicate effectively with each other. Can you think of five reasons why this is important?

▶ Working together to meet objectives

The public services work together to meet their objectives and to manage their spending, as shown in Table 1.9.

Table 1.9: How public services work together.

Working together to...	Description
Manage spending	• Allows the services to spend public money wisely and reduce expenditure where possible. This is important because the services are paid for by the public through taxation. • Responsibilities can be shared and collective influence can be used to negotiate the best deals.
Meet the public service organisation's objectives	• Each service sets itself a series of objectives. • Some objectives cannot be achieved without teamwork with other public services, e.g. if a local authority sets itself an objective to reduce anti-social behaviour, it will have to work with the police to achieve this.
Meet performance measures set by government	• Central government often sets targets for the public services which they must achieve, e.g. the Ambulance Service has response time targets (see page 7). • The Ambulance Service can only meet these targets if staff at the local hospital work effectively with ambulance crews to admit patients to hospital for treatment and free up the ambulance to continue to its next emergency.

The consequences of not working together can be serious for the public services and for the public whom they serve. It can cost time, money and even lives. Some negative impacts of services failing to work together are shown in Figure 1.3.

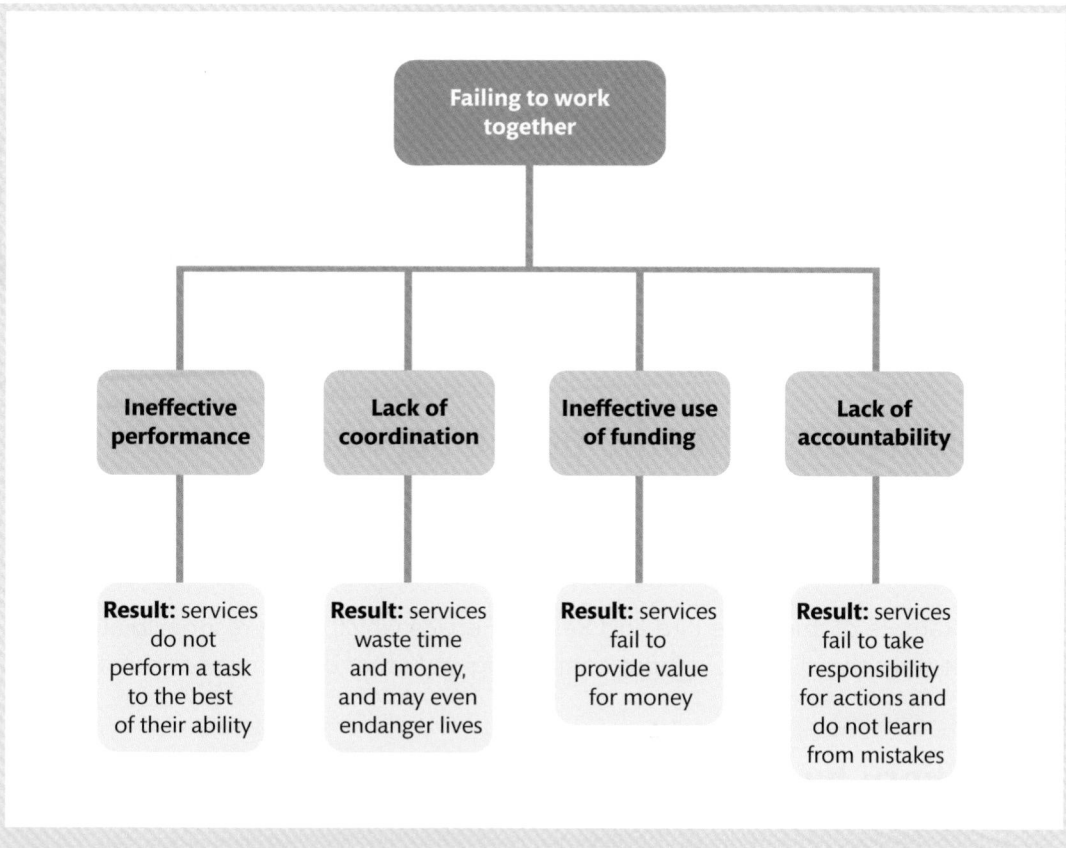

Figure 1.3: The negative impacts of services failing to work together.

Assessment practice 1.4

A major road traffic incident has occurred on the M1 motorway. There are 14 known casualties, many of whom are still trapped in vehicles.

1 Identify the **three** services that would be most likely to arrive first on the scene. [3]

2 Name the service that would be responsible for rerouting traffic and ensuring other motorists can continue on their journey. [1]

3 Explain why effective communication between the services is essential in this situation. [2]

4 Explain why it is important to protect the scene of the incident. [1]

5 Give **two** reasons why people would not be allowed to gather and watch the incident. [2]

▶ How public services are delivered

Introduction

Public services can be delivered in a number of different ways by a number of different organisations. There are advantages and disadvantages to all of the delivery models used. Can you think of a service that is provided by a charity? What are the advantages and disadvantages of this?

▷ Delivery by a specific public service

Delivery by a specific public service is a very simple delivery model where the public service in question takes complete and direct responsibility for the delivery of a particular service.

A good example of this is the Fire and Rescue Service which has a responsibility to put out fires. It does this directly, without contracting any other companies or services to assist it.

▷ Delivery by the private or voluntary sectors

The public services often find that it is more cost-effective to contract out a service to a charity or a private sector company than to deliver it themselves. Commonly contracted-out services include refuse collection and adult social care. Private companies and charities are often able to deliver these services cheaply as they do not have the overheads of a public service.

Public services such as local authorities will issue an invitation to **tender** for the service. Public services are required to be fair and open in their tendering process to ensure that it is a truly competitive process and that one particular company is not being favoured over others.

Key term

Tender – a bid or proposal. It contains information on how a company would deliver the service being put out to tender and how much it would charge for doing this.

▷ Partnership delivery

Partnership delivery is where groups of services, voluntary sector organisations and private companies come together to deliver a service in partnership. Since the early 1990s, health care in the UK has been delivered extensively through partnership arrangements, with over 130 projects completed with a value of £12 billion.

Common arrangements include private finance initiatives (PFI) where private sector money is used to fund and build hospitals and schools. The private company is then allowed to charge rent and maintenance for a long period after the building is complete. This has the advantage of not having to increase taxation to pay for buildings, but it ties hospitals and schools into rent and maintenance contracts for very long periods of time.

Advantages and disadvantages of partnership delivery

There are always advantages and disadvantages to any delivery model in the public services.

The **advantages** of partnership delivery include the following points.

- Costs can be shared between partners. A project that might have been too expensive for one service should be afforded by several working in partnership.
- Expertise and knowledge can be shared. Bringing together the expertise of public, private and voluntary sector organisations can strengthen a project.
- Projects can be completed more efficiently by working together and sharing expertise and resources.
- Organisations can share their knowledge of updates to important information, such as government directives, and this can make them more effective.

The **disadvantages** of partnership delivery include the following points.

- It can be very expensive and time-consuming to set up and run projects involving multiple partners. It can also take time to find partners prepared to work with the services.
- Communication can be difficult, especially as different partners have different viewpoints and ideas. Agreeing contracts or plans can be challenging. Communication problems can delay or even stop a project.
- Coordinating meetings between multiple partners can be very difficult.
- If the project or service goes wrong, it is the responsibility of the public service and not their private sector partners.
- Public and private sector organisations can have different priorities, because the public sector aims to serve the public while private sector organisations usually focus on profit. Sometimes, these two different goals may conflict.

Just checking

1 What is a tender?
2 What is partnership delivery?
3 Give one advantage and one disadvantage of partnership delivery.

▶ How public services are funded

Introduction

Have you ever wondered how the public services are funded? Or how much a particular service costs to run? Have you ever considered whether the services offer value for money? All of these questions are really important at the moment as the government needs to save money.

▶ Emergency services

Emergency services are primarily funded by grants from central government. However, they can also be funded by money from the local authority and sometimes through private or corporate donations. They can also take out loans to fund capital projects, or work in partnership with the private sector.

Central government allocates a certain amount of money each year for a service to use. This is its budget. If the budget is not enough then the service either needs to find other ways of raising money or to operate its service in a cheaper way. The money is allocated by taking into account the size of the service's local population. This is intended to make the allocation of money to each area or service as fair as possible, and can lead to different services being allocated very different amounts of money.

Activity 1.5   Allocating funds

In 2013–14, the following Police Services were allocated the following funds from central government:

- Cumbria £65.8 million
- South Yorkshire £194.9 million
- Warwickshire £53.4 million
- West Midlands £472.8 million
- Greater London £1.95 billion.

1 Why does each Police Service have a different amount of money allocated to it?
2 What are the factors that the government takes into account when allocating money to services?
3 Research the sizes of these Police Services. Do you think these allocations are fair? Explain your answer.

▶ Armed services

The armed services are always directly funded by central government. This is because the armed services do not belong to one geographical region of the country as local authorities or emergency services do. The armed services have two separate budgets:

1 a general budget which covers operational duties and all associated costs
2 a capital budget which covers the costs of equipment.

The armed services spend heavily on equipment and this spending must be planned years in advance. This is because aircraft carriers, aircraft, ships and submarines are made to order by specialised companies, and they can take years to design, build and test.

Case study

In 2012, a £1.2 billion contract was announced to design, construct, test and commission a new attack submarine called Audacious. Audacious is the fourth in a series of seven brand new Astute class submarines bought by the Royal Navy, which includes HMS Astute and HMS Ambush. The contract secured 3,000 jobs in Cumbria, where the submarines are built.

HMS Astute was the first submarine in the Astute class and she took several years to build. The actual build for Audacious began in 2009 and items for her construction were ordered as early as 2007. She is due to enter service as HMS Audacious in 2018.

HMS Ambush

1 Why do the armed services need a separate budget for equipment?

2 Why does it take so long for some equipment to be ordered and built?

3 What would be the impact of not providing our armed services with the latest equipment?

4 Why is it important to spend time testing equipment such as submarines before they go into service?

▶ Central government

Central government receives its income by taxing individuals, companies, goods and services. There are a number of different types of tax which generate income for the government, as shown in Table 1.10.

Table 1.10: Forms of taxation.

Tax	Description
Corporation tax	Claimed by the government from the profits of companies that operate in the UK.
Value Added Tax (VAT)	Charged on most goods and services provided by businesses in the UK.
Income tax	Taken from the personal income of members of the public. The rate at which you pay is dependent on how much you earn (i.e. the higher your salary, the more income tax you pay).
Inheritance tax	Taken from money and property received as an **inheritance**.

Did you know?

In 2012–13, corporation tax raised £39.5 billion for HM Treasury.

Key term

Inheritance – the passing on of property, titles or money after someone has died.

Local authorities

Local authorities get a proportion of their income from central government. They also collect taxes, including:

- council tax – a tax on households, based on the value of the property and how many people live there
- business rates – taxes charged on properties such as shops, pubs and offices, which do not fall under council tax.

Many local authorities also charge for services such as leisure centres.

Voluntary services or the third sector

Charities sometimes receive grants from central government, but they normally have to rely on public donations, business sponsorship or **legacies** from wills.

Charities can also conduct fundraising activities which help to raise awareness of particular issues as well as generate income. Large fundraising events include:

- Race for Life – over £50 million raised in 2013 to fight cancer
- Children in Need – £31 million raised in 2013 to combat disadvantage and poverty for children and young people in the UK
- Red Nose Day – over £100 million raised in 2013 to support aid work in the UK and overseas.

Key term

Legacy – an amount of money or property left to someone in a will.

More ways of raising income

Public services can also raise money by other means, as shown in Table 1.11.

Table 1.11: Methods of raising income for public services.

Method	Description
Public private partnerships	Public and private sector organisations share the costs of running a service.
Contracted-out services	A public service allows a third party to deliver a service on its behalf, usually for a reduced cost. The public service retains accountability.
Direct charges	A public service charges for certain services. Examples include a local authority charging for car parking or the NHS charging for prescription drugs.

Impact of funding on service delivery

Introduction

Have you ever wanted to do something and not had enough money? When funding to the public services is cut, it has an impact on the work they can do. Think of a public service and consider which parts of their job they might have to prioritise if budgets are tightened.

Although having less money does not always mean a reduction in service levels, it can change how the service delivers its statutory and non-statutory services.

As discussed earlier, statutory services must be provided by law, whereas non-statutory services are provided to support the statutory services. However, when funding is reduced, the non-statutory services will be cut or reduced first. For example, local authorities will protect front line statutory services such as children's services and adult social care, but as a result they have to save money elsewhere on services such as libraries.

The level, extent and quality of service

The amount of funding received by a public service determines the level, extent and quality of service it provides. However, it does not always follow that just because a service has more money it will deliver a better service. Sometimes, reduced funding can lead to finding **innovative** ways of delivering a service, which might actually be better than previous systems.

Some public services have changed their staffing mix to reduce costs and employ less expensive staff. For example, the MOD plans to decrease the number of regular soldiers in the Army and increase the number of volunteers in the Army Reserve. In the Police Service, Special Constables and Police Community Support Officers (PCSOs) are used as a more cost-effective way of supplementing regular police officers.

 Key term

Innovative – new or different ways of doing things.

Some services are using less expensive staff, such as PCSOs, as part of their cost saving measures. What do you think about this?

Take it further

Use the NHS website to find out more about who is entitled to free prescriptions in England.

Charging for public services

Not everything the public services do can be provided free of charge. There simply is not enough money to supply entire communities with everything they might want. This means that some services have to be paid for at point of access. For example, it is standard to be charged for prescriptions and dental work, although individuals who cannot afford to pay for these services may be exempt.

Allocating public services

Not everyone needs the same public services at the same time. Some people rarely need to have contact with the services, while others have extensive contact with them. This means that the public services are allocated to people based on need. For example, if you need an ambulance, then one will be sent to you. If you do not need a service, it will be allocated to someone in greater need elsewhere.

As a result, some people feel that the system is unfair, because some people pay more in and take less out while others pay less in and take more out.

Public services can be allocated in different ways, such as:

- **universal access** – the service is free for the public to use (e.g. GP appointments)
- **means testing** – individuals have their income assessed and receive the service if their income falls below a specified amount (e.g. free prescriptions for people on very low incomes in England)
- **charging** – individuals are charged directly for a particular public service (e.g. car parking in local authority car parks).

Discussion

The public services provide many of their services for free as they are already paid for by the public through their taxes. Do you think that the public services should start charging people on higher incomes for more of their services?

Assessment practice 1.5

1 Name **three** taxes that central government uses to raise money. [3]

2 A local authority has had a budget cut of 3% and needs to save money on the services it provides or raise additional money from other sources.

   a Explain **one** way the local authority could cut its spending. [2]

   b Explain **one** way in which the local authority could increase its income. [2]

▶ Accountability in public service delivery

Introduction

The public services often seem like the people in charge, not the public, but actually the relationship is the other way around. The public fund the services by paying taxes, and this means that the services are held accountable to the public and other groups. What do you think accountability means? Can you think of an example where you have been unhappy with the performance of a public service? What could you do about it?

▷ Accountability

Accountability means being answerable for a set of actions or decisions. It means that representatives of a service can be placed under public **scrutiny** and asked to explain their actions or decisions.

The public services have to be accountable because they are paid for by the public through taxes. This means that the public has a right to know how the money is being spent, so that they can have confidence in the service. This also ensures transparency, which prevents fraud and corruption. Most services produce an annual report which details exactly what they have done and why, which also helps to promote public confidence.

▷ What are the services accountable for?

The public services are accountable for the key aspects of their work, including those outlined below.

- **Finances and budgets** – the services must be accountable for how they spend the money that is given to them and how well they manage their budgets.
- **Service provision** – the services are accountable for the level and quality of the service they deliver to the public. They have a clear **remit** given to them by the government or set by their own objectives, and they are held accountable for the services they must provide.
- **Legal compliance** – public services must do some things by law, and these are known as their statutory duties (see pages 16–17). For example, a local authority has a statutory duty to properly manage social housing, and the Fire and Rescue Service has a statutory duty to put out fires.

▷ Who are the services accountable to?

The public services are accountable to a range of organisations and individuals, including government, regulators and the public.

Key terms

Scrutiny – the process of examining something very carefully.

Remit – a task or set of jobs given to an individual or organisation.

Key term

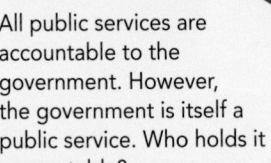

Parliament – the body of people and organisations which governs a country. In the UK, this is made up of the king or queen, the House of Commons and the House of Lords.

Discussion

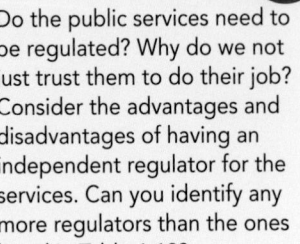

All public services are accountable to the government. However, the government is itself a public service. Who holds it accountable?

Discussion

Do the public services need to be regulated? Why do we not just trust them to do their job? Consider the advantages and disadvantages of having an independent regulator for the services. Can you identify any more regulators than the ones listed in Table 1.12?

Government and parliament

All public services are ultimately accountable to central government and **parliament** for their conduct and performance. This is because central government sets targets and statutory responsibilities for the public sector and provides the services with the money they need to do their job.

Regulators

Regulators are organisations which check that the public services are doing their job to the required standard, and are providing high-quality service and value for money. The regulators can also penalise services which have underperformed. Table 1.12 shows some examples of regulators.

Table 1.12: Examples of regulators and their roles.

Regulator	Role
Her Majesty's Inspectorate of Constabulary	Independently assesses police forces and policing activities from neighbourhood policing to serious crime and the fight against terrorism.
Care Quality Commission	Ensures that hospitals, care homes, dental and GP surgeries, and other care services in the UK provide safe and high-quality care to patients.
Ofsted	Inspects and regulates services which care for children and young people, as well as those providing education and training for learners of all ages. This includes nurseries, childcare providers, schools and colleges.

The public

The public pay for the public services through taxation. Although the services are not directly responsible to the entire British public, they are responsible to the public's elected representatives in the House of Commons (our MPs).

Assessment practice 1.6

The police are accountable for their performance to the government who will monitor their performance and inspect them regularly. They are also accountable to the public who can make complaints against the Police Service to the Independent Police Complaints Commission (IPCC). These complaints must be investigated.

1 Name the organisation or body to which the armed services are accountable. [1]

2 Explain why it is important that the services are accountable. [1]

3 Explain why it is important that the services are transparent. [1]

WorkSpace

▶ Lance Corporal Kelly Stevens

Army Reserve

I work as part of 38 Signals Regiment, which is an Army Reserve regiment with responsibility for providing information and communication systems to the emergency services and local government in an emergency. We can also be deployed overseas with regular soldiers. We can be called upon to do a variety of things – for example, our Brigade has been involved in dealing with firefighter strikes, foot and mouth disease and responding to severe flooding.

There is no such thing as a typical day in the Army Reserve. When we are on camp we may be involved in a variety of activities, including battle simulations, working with other NATO forces from different countries, and repairing and maintaining equipment. The Army Reserve are an essential support to the regular army and we have to make sure we are prepared to be deployed if we are called upon.

I love my job with the Army Reserve – not only is it very different from my day job, but I also get the chance to contribute to the safety and security of our nation, which is a tremendous responsibility. The teamwork and camaraderie of the unit is excellent and I have met people from all walks of life who share the same goals as I do. I'm proud to be a part of the Army Reserve.

Think about it

1 What topics have you covered in this unit so far which might give you the knowledge to understand what an Army Reserve soldier does?

2 What skills and knowledge do you think you need to develop further if you want to be involved in the British Army in the future?

3 How do the Army Reserve and the regular army work together to ensure the defence of the nation?

Assessment Zone

This section has been written to help you to do your best when you take the assessment test. Read through it carefully and ask your tutor if there is anything you are still not sure about.

How you will be assessed

For this unit you will be assessed through a one-hour written examination. The examination paper will have a maximum of 50 marks. The number of marks available for each part of a question will be shown in brackets, e.g. [2], with the total for each question being shown at the end of the question.

There will be different types of questions in the examination:

A Questions where all of the answers are available and you have to choose the correct answer(s). *Tip: Always read the instructions carefully. Sometimes you may need to identify more than one correct answer.*

Examples:

Public services can be grouped by the type of work they do. Identify the **two** services from the following list that are voluntary. [2]

A The Police Service

B Victim Support

C HM Prison Service

D The Royal Marines

E British Red Cross

Answers: B and E

Identify the statement which best describes how the emergency services are funded. [1]

A Mainly from tax

B Mainly from donations

C Mainly from charging for their services

Answer: A

B Questions where you are asked to produce a short answer worth 1 or 2 marks. *Tip: Look carefully at how the question is set out to see how many points need to be included in your answer.*

Examples:

Tax is a charge made by the government for the services it provides.

Name two types of tax that the government uses to raise money. [2]

Possible answers: Corporation tax, inheritance tax, income tax, council tax or business rates.

Disclaimer: These practice questions and sample answers are not actual exam questions. They are provided as a practice aid only and should not be assumed to reflect the format or coverage of the real external test.

> Name two public services for which the Ministry of Defence is responsible. [2]
>
> **Possible answers:** RAF, Royal Navy, British Army, Royal Marines.

C **Questions where you are asked to provide a longer answer – these can be worth up to 8 marks.** *Tips: Make sure that you read the question in full and answer all the parts of the question. It is a good idea to plan your answer so that you do not forget anything. Remember to check your answer once you have finished.*

Example:

> The government has allocated spending for public services up to and including 2016 as part of its budgeting process. Spending has been protected on three public services: international aid, education and the NHS. All other government departments have had to take a cut in funding of around 3% per year.
>
> Discuss the implications of this cut in funding on the public services. [8]
>
> **Answer:**
>
> In general, the implications of this funding cut fall into two categories:
>
> **1.** the public services have to cut their costs
>
> **2.** the public services have to increase their income.
>
> If the public services need to cut the costs of the services they deliver, they need to explore new ways of delivering what they do so they can save money. One way they could do this is to contract out some of their services. Contracting out is when a public service allows part of its duties to be delivered by a private company or a charity. Sometimes private companies can deliver services for less money, because they have fewer overheads.
>
> Funding cuts also have an implication for staffing. Well-trained and well-equipped public servants are expensive. Costs could be cut by changing the mix of staffing to include cheaper alternatives – for example, Army Reserve soldiers or Police Community Support Officers.
>
> The other option that public services have is to increase their income. This could be done in a number of ways. For example, a local authority could increase local taxes such as business rates or council tax to increase their income in order to deliver the services they need. However, this would not be popular.
>
> Another way to increase income is to increase the number of things the services charge for and charge more for services they already charge for. This could include services like car parking or policing football matches. The public services might have to look for more services they could sell, as well as increasing the cost of things they already offer.

Hints and tips

- **Use the time before the test.** Make sure that you have everything you will need. Check that your pens work and that you have read the instructions on the front of your examination paper. Try to make yourself feel comfortable and relaxed.

- **Keep an eye on the time.** The examination will last one hour, and you should be able to see the clock in the examination room so that you know how long you have got left to complete the paper. As a rough guide, allow one minute for every mark on the paper. This means that a question worth five marks should take you around five minutes to complete.

- **Read the questions fully.** Make sure you read each question through enough times to make sure that you understand what you are being asked to do. It is easy to misread a question and then write an answer which is wrong. Check that you are doing what you are being asked to do.

- **Plan your answers.** For longer questions, it is worth spending a minute or two to write down the key points which you want to include in your answer. If you are being asked to evaluate, you will need to think about positive and negative points. Using a plan will allow you to make sure you include both in your answer.

- **Check your answers.** Once you have answered all of the questions on the paper, you will probably have a few minutes to spare. Use this time to check your answers and fill in any blanks which you have left. Try to answer every question on the paper.

- **Read through longer answers.** Read through your longer answers to make sure your answer makes sense, and you have answered the question fully.

- **Make sure you have filled out the front of the paper.** Once the examination has ended, check that you have written your name and candidate number on the front of the paper. This is important so that you will gain the marks for your work.

How to improve your answer

Read the two student answers below, together with the feedback.

Try to use what you learn here to improve your answers in your examination.

▶ Question

Public services often work in partnership with each other to deliver services to the public.

Explain two advantages and one challenge of the public services working together as a team. [6]

▶ Student 1's answer

Advantage 1 – saves money.

Advantage 2 – saves lives.

Challenge 1 – communication is difficult.

Feedback:

Student 1 has identified the correct advantages and challenge, which receive 1 mark each. However, the student hasn't explained why they have come up with these answers. This student needs to explain why lives and money would be saved and why communication is difficult when the services work together. Overall, Student 1 receives 3 marks for this answer.

▶ Student 2's answer

Advantage 1 – saves money. By working together, public services can save money by coordinating their activities so they each know what they are responsible for, and by sharing information which might save another service a lot of work. They can also buy things together which saves money.

Advantage 2 – saves lives. If the public services work well together, they can respond faster to emergencies. Faster responses mean that more lives can be saved. For example, at the scene of a traffic incident, the three main emergency services know what their jobs are and they get on with them quickly and effectively. If they did not train together and understand each other there would be chaos.

Challenge 1 – communication is difficult. It can be hard for different services to communicate clearly with each other during a serious incident. For example, if there is flooding, communication would have to be very good between all three emergency services, the local authority and charities helping the people who have been rescued, and even the armed services if they are supporting.

Feedback:

Student 2 has identified each advantage and given reasons and examples (they receive 2 marks for each advantage with reasons). They have also correctly identified a challenge and explained it, providing a scenario to illustrate their point (another 2 marks). Overall, Student 2 receives 6 marks in total for this answer.

Assess yourself

Question 1

Which two of the following responsibilities belong to the Fire and Rescue Service? [2]

A Putting out fires   **C** Fire safety education

B Defending the nation   **D** Arresting people

Question 2

The local authority provides over 700 services to the public, including libraries and rubbish collection.

Name two other services provided by the local authority. [2]

▶ Question 3

Ben is a new recruit to the Fire and Rescue Service. As part of his training, he has to understand the roles and responsibilities of the other services he will work with.

Identify the services Ben is most likely to come into contact with and discuss how those services work with the Fire and Rescue Service. [8]

Introduction

Developing the skills for working in the public sector can be quite a challenge. The public services deal with a wide range of situations on a day-to-day basis, some of which involve the most difficult circumstances you will encounter in any job.

If you were policing a demonstration and some of the demonstrators became aggressive, how would you work to calm the situation and keep your colleagues and the public safe? If you were a charity worker at a large charity event, how would you cooperate with other staff to manage the movement of people? What skills would you need to do these jobs?

Public service work is incredibly demanding, but it is also incredibly rewarding. The most successful public servants often feel a genuine need to give something back to the community and help others to be safe or to make a better life for themselves. This unit will help you identify and develop the skills you need in any public service to meet the needs of the people you serve.

Assessment: This unit will be assessed through a series of assignments set by your tutor/teacher.

Learning aims

In this unit you will:

A explore working skills used in the public service sector

B demonstrate working skills used in the public service sector.

I didn't realise all the skills you need to work in the public services. You have to be able to communicate with people who might be angry, upset or scared, and you have to do this while you might be angry or scared yourself. I think the skills I have learned in this unit are useful for any job, not just those in the public services.

Samuel, *14-year-old Public Services student*

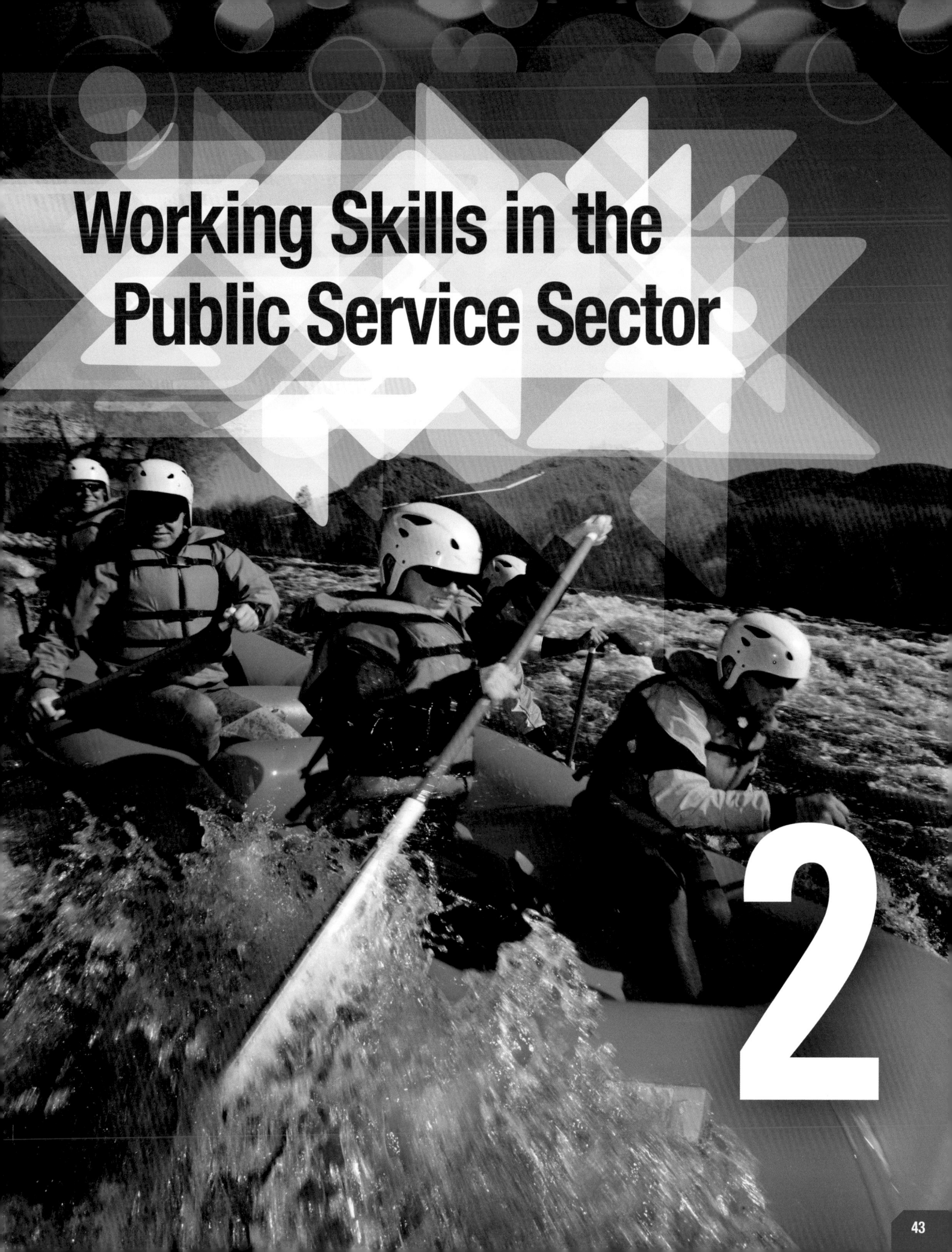

Working Skills in the Public Service Sector

2

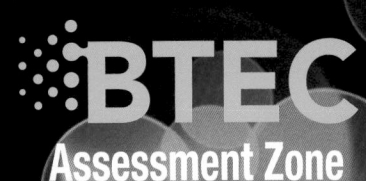

BTEC Assessment Zone

This table shows you what you must do in order to achieve a **Pass**, **Merit** or **Distinction** grade, and where you can find activities to help you.

Assessment criteria

Level 1	Level 2 Pass	Level 2 Merit	Level 2 Distinction
Learning aim A: Explore working skills used in the public service sector			
1A.1 Identify internal and external customers of two contrasting public services.	**2A.P1** Describe internal and external customers of two contrasting public services. **See Assessment activity 2.1, page 59**	**2A.M1** Explain how customer needs are met in two contrasting public services. **See Assessment activity 2.1, page 59**	**2A.D1** English Assess how working skills are used by two contrasting public services to meet customer needs. **See Assessment activity 2.1, page 59**
1A.2 English Describe working skills used with customers by two contrasting public services.	**2A.P2** English Explain working skills used with customers by two contrasting public services. **See Assessment activity 2.1, page 59**	**2A.M2** English Compare working skills used with customers by two contrasting public services. **See Assessment activity 2.1, page 59**	
Learning aim B: Demonstrate working skills used in the public service sector			
1B.3 Demonstrate own working skills through teamwork in a public service situation.	**2B.P3** Demonstrate own working skills through teamwork in two contrasting public service situations. **See Assessment activity 2.2, page 64**	**2B.M3** Compare own performance as a team member in two contrasting public service situations in terms of strengths and areas for improvement. **See Assessment activity 2.2, page 64**	**2B.D2** English Assess own performance as a team member in two contrasting public service situations and develop an action plan for improvements. **See Assessment activity 2.2, page 64**
1B.4 Outline own performance of working skills through teamwork in a public service situation.	**2B.P4** Describe own performance as a team member in two contrasting public service situations. **See Assessment activity 2.2, page 64**		

English Opportunity to practise English skills

How you will be assessed

This unit will be assessed by a series of assignments set by your tutor. You will need to explore the type of skills used in public service work, such as communication and teamwork, in order to meet the needs of a variety of customers.

You will also be expected to demonstrate these skills in practice and to consider your own performance in those skills and identify areas where you might need to improve.

Your assignment could be in the form of:

- role plays
- video recordings
- presentations
- written reports.

Meeting the needs of public services customers

Introduction

If you work in the public services you are a public servant. Your customers are the general public and you need to meet their needs. The general public is very diverse in terms of language, culture and background. Your customers also include your colleagues and people in other public services. How can public service workers meet the different needs of all these individuals?

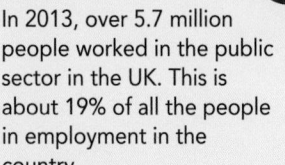

Did you know?

In 2013, over 5.7 million people worked in the public sector in the UK. This is about 19% of all the people in employment in the country.

Internal customers

Internal customers are those who work in your organisation or in other organisations which you have to help.

Colleagues

Your colleagues are your customers, and you have to ensure that you do your job properly so they can do theirs. If you do not give them the information and support they need, you may make them underperform. As a result, the whole organisation may underperform.

Supervisors and senior managers

Your supervisors and senior managers are also your customers. They set clear tasks to be done which help the organisation as a whole, and you have a responsibility to carry out those tasks.

Remember that they are held accountable, just as you are. If you do not deliver what they have asked of you, they will not be able to deliver what their managers have asked of them.

Staff in other public services

The public services do not work in isolation. In order to do their jobs, they have to work in partnership with lots of different organisations. For example, at the scene of a major incident, all three emergency services work alongside each other as well as other services such as the local authority and support services. Each service has to do their job in order for the other services to do theirs.

External customers

External customers are the individuals and groups who are not employed by the public services and who use the services that your organisation provides. They are generally the public users of a service and are what most public servants consider to be their primary customers.

External users can be divided into two groups:

- existing service users, who have used the service before
- new service users, who have not used the service before.

We use some services very frequently, such as schools, colleges or the NHS, and we are often very familiar with these. However, there are other services which we only use when we have a problem, such as the Police Service or the Fire and Rescue Service. Organisations that serve the public have to be able to deal with members of the public who may be frightened or stressed.

Different groups of service users

Public service organisations will come into contact with all kinds of individuals and groups during the course of their working day, as shown in Figure 2.1. These different groups and individuals will have a wide range of needs and the services need to be able to respond appropriately to them.

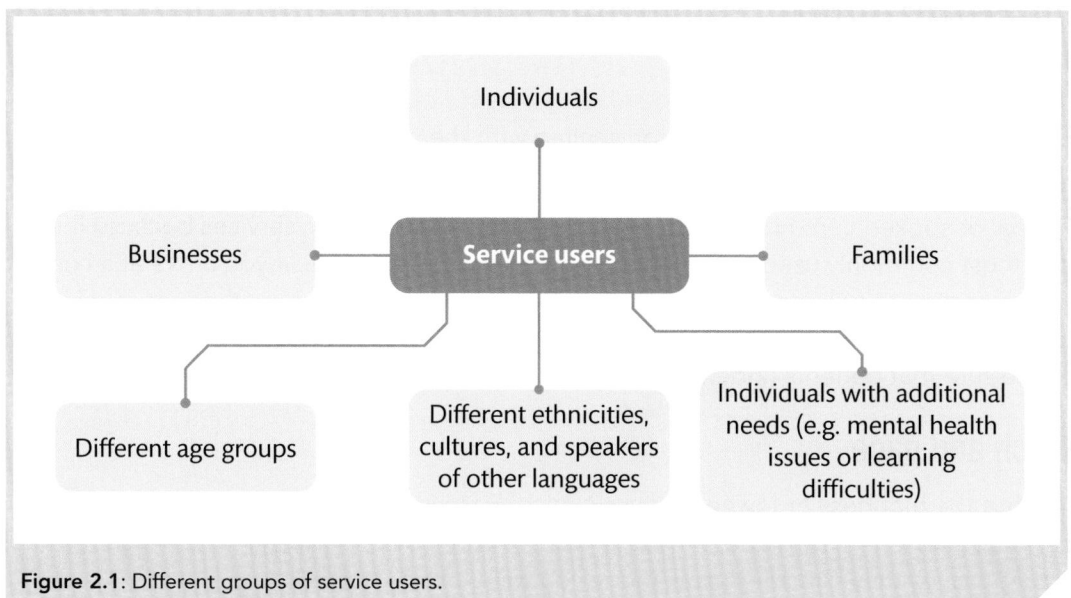

Figure 2.1: Different groups of service users.

Activity 2.1   **Who are your customers?**

Choose a public service and identify:

- three internal customers of the service
- three external customers of the service
- four different groups of people who might use the service.

▶ Working skills within public service sector groups

Introduction

The public services have to be able to deal with the different needs of lots of different customers. What differences do you think there might be between a police officer and a local authority worker, or a nurse and a firefighter? Each of them deals with the public in a slightly different way and needs a slightly different skill set.

Key terms

Blue light services – the main emergency services: Police, Fire and Rescue and Ambulance Services and HM Coastguard.

Third sector – another name for the voluntary sector.

The different public services are the emergency services (**blue light services**), armed services, local government, central government and the voluntary sector (**third sector**). They must use appropriate communication skills with customers of the public services, including speaking, listening and writing skills.

▶ Speaking skills

The voice is a very powerful tool for dealing with the public, especially when you use different tones and methods of emphasising words.

Verbal or spoken communication is very important in the public services because it is the most commonly used form of communication. For example, if you arrive at a crime scene and meet a distressed victim, you need to be able to speak with them calmly until support arrives. If you work in a doctor's surgery or on a hospital ward, you need to make sure that patients understand any important information you tell them.

Remember

- Even when you are under pressure, it is important that you speak clearly and calmly, or you may be misunderstood.
- The way in which you say something is just as important as what you say.

Pitch and pace

Pitch is the highness or lowness of your voice. Pace is the speed at which you speak. It is important to control the pitch and pace of your voice, especially in emergency situations, as they can affect how easily you will be understood.

Tone

Tone is the way in which we speak, and this shapes the meaning of what we say. The tone of our voice and the way in which we emphasise words can make the things we say mean different things. Even the same sentence said in a different way can take on a different meaning.

Discussion

Have you ever said something and the person you were speaking to completely misunderstood? In small groups discuss situations where you were misunderstood. Consider how the misunderstanding happened and what you could do to prevent it happening again.

Activity 2.2   Tone of voice

Can you think of an example where the same sentence could mean different things depending on the tone of the speaker? Consider the sentence below:

"I love visiting art galleries and museums."

How would you change the tone of your voice to mean exactly the opposite of what the sentence is saying? How do you detect this kind of difference in tone when people are speaking to you?

By varying the volume of what we say, we can communicate emotions and feelings. We can shout, whisper, talk gently or sternly, all of which gives an insight into how we are feeling.

We often change how we speak according to who is listening. You may use different language with your friends than with a stranger or a person in authority. Other factors that influence the way we speak might be the age of the listener, the subject matter or the situation that we are in. For example, if you were attending an interview you would speak politely, avoiding any **slang** or **jargon**. You would use a calm, formal tone to show that you can stay calm under pressure. In comparison, when talking to your friends, your tone and language would probably be more relaxed.

You should avoid using slang or jargon in some situations, because not everyone will understand what you mean and it can get in the way of effective communication. For example, at the scene of a road traffic incident, it is very important that the senior police officer in charge does not use jargon or slang that other professionals or the public do not understand. If they do, instructions may be misunderstood and lives may be put in danger.

▶ Listening skills

Listening skills are very important in daily life, especially in the public services. You will need to have good listening skills when attending a briefing or a meeting, answering questions or dealing with a complaint or request. The people you are listening to may be in distress, upset or scared, and it may be difficult to understand what they are saying. There may be loud background noise, such as sirens or shouting. This means that you must concentrate in order to listen to the speaker and gain their trust. This may even help to calm the situation.

Being attentive

Attentiveness is a key listening skill. Vital information can be picked up at any time in a conversation, so it is important that you pay attention to what is being said and do not let your mind wander. You should never talk over the person you are listening to, as this may discourage them from opening up to you.

Repeating back important information

Repeating back important information can be a useful tactic. Sometimes, when you have to take in lots of complex or technical information, you may need to check that you have understood the message clearly. Do this by repeating back the key points and asking the person you are speaking with to confirm that you have the right message.

Key terms

Slang – words that you use informally (i.e. you and your friend/colleague may know what it means, but others would not).

Jargon – this means words and phrases that are used specifically within an organisation, such as 'blues and twos' for the lights on police cars or 'fence' to describe a person to whom stolen goods are sold.

Did you know?

999 handles over 30 million calls per year. Dealing efficiently with this volume of emergency calls requires excellent communication skills.

Discussion

How do you know if someone is not paying attention to you when you are speaking? Work in small groups and discuss the body language and other clues you pick up on if someone is not interested in what you have to say.

Making notes

Discussion

Can you think of any other situations where making notes might be important?

Making notes while you are receiving information can be a good idea, so that you have a record of the conversation and do not forget what was said. This may be useful if you need to pass the information on to other public services. For example, if you are taking a police statement from a witness, victim or suspect, you will need to record this information accurately as the statement may form the basis of a future court case. Your listening and writing skills have to be really good so that the statements you take can stand up to scrutiny in court.

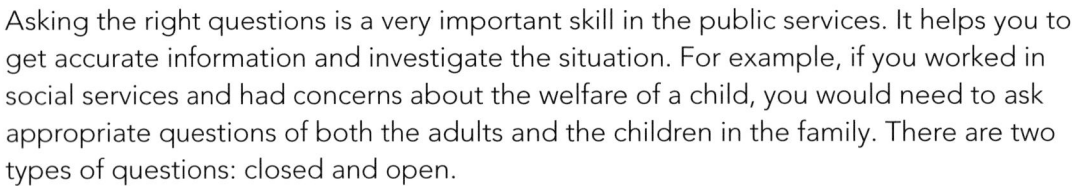

Activity 2.3   **Pass it on**

As a whole group, sit in a circle. Your tutor will whisper an order into one person's ear. That person will then whisper into the ear of the person to their left and so on until the order reaches the last person. This person will then come to the front of the class and write the order on the board.

Has the order changed? Discuss what happened and try to identify what went wrong with your listening and communication skills.

Asking appropriate questions

Asking the right questions is a very important skill in the public services. It helps you to get accurate information and investigate the situation. For example, if you worked in social services and had concerns about the welfare of a child, you would need to ask appropriate questions of both the adults and the children in the family. There are two types of questions: closed and open.

- **Closed questions** – you would expect a short answer from a closed question. They usually begin with a verb such as 'Did', 'Are', 'Have' or 'Do', for example, 'Did you go to college today?'
- **Open questions** – these usually begin with verbs such as 'Where', 'What', 'Why', or 'Who'. They encourage the person who is answering to speak at length. It is difficult to give a simple 'yes' or 'no' reply to an open question. For example, 'What is your opinion on public service funding cuts?' is an open question.

▶ Body language

What type of body language does each of these photos show?

Body language is our posture, or the way we stand or sit. A person's body language can often communicate more than their spoken words – it can tell you whether they are angry or sad, relaxed or anxious. For example, if someone has their arms folded, it might indicate that they are feeling nervous because their body language is 'closed'.

If you use relaxed and 'open' body language, other people may feel more comfortable around you and may trust you more. This can help you in many situations.

Gestures and facial expressions

We use hand gestures and facial expressions to communicate how we feel or to emphasise a point. For example, when you are happy you smile, and when you do not like something you may frown. If you need to emphasise something you are saying, you could use hand gestures.

Appropriate eye contact

Eye contact is a very important tool in the public services. If you look at someone while speaking to them, it implies that you are honest and have nothing to hide. It is also useful when you are having trouble making yourself understood verbally. However, remember that there is a big difference between making eye contact and staring at someone, which is considered rude.

If you are wearing sunglasses or a visor, this can create a barrier between you and the person you are speaking to. It's best to remove these to help create a sense of trust and understanding.

 Did you know?

In some cultures, making eye contact can be considered inappropriate.

Activity 2.4   Observing body language

1 Working in pairs, go to a busy place in your school or college, such as reception or the canteen. Consider the types of body language you can see.

2 Try watching your favourite TV programme for 10 minutes with the sound turned off. Can you still understand what is going on?

3 How did the body language you observed inform you about the situations in your school or college, or in the TV programme?

▶ Styles of communication

As a member of the public services you will have to communicate in lots of different ways with colleagues, with other services and with the public. It is important to know how to choose the most appropriate method for the situation. Different ways to communicate include:

- face-to-face
- on the telephone
- in writing (such as letter, email and fax).

Face-to-face communication

✓ This is the best method of communication, because you can read an individual's body language and tone of voice, and this helps you to understand how to deal with the situation.

✓ The person you are dealing with can also read your body language and your tone of voice, which may make it easier to resolve the situation.

✗ It takes time to speak with everyone you need to deal with on an individual basis, and there are quicker and cheaper ways to communicate.

Did you know?

Fax is an older technology used to communicate written information via telephone lines. It is still used by some public services, but is gradually being superseded by email.

Telephone communication

✓ This allows you to communicate directly without needing to be in the same location as the other person, so it saves time and money.

✓ You can still hear and respond to tone of voice, and clarify any misunderstandings as you go along.

✗ You lose the ability to use body language, which means that it may be easier to misinterpret the message.

Written communication

✓ Letters are good for communicating formal non-urgent information, such as the date of a routine hospital appointment.

✓ Emails are cheap to send and arrive almost instantaneously.

✗ Letters are costly to send and can be slow to arrive.

✗ All forms of written communication can be read in ways that were not intended (this also includes other text-based communications, including text messages, tweets and Facebook messages).

Activity 2.5   Choosing styles of communication

You are a local government officer and need to decide the best styles of communication to use when responding to each of the following situations.

1 A member of the public has made a formal complaint about their bins not being emptied for a month.

2 A member of your team has been late to work all week. They are normally very reliable and you are concerned that something may be wrong.

3 You need to ensure a list of housing repairs reaches the appropriate department.

4 You need to give your line manager a quick update on a budget issue.

State which method of communication you would use in each situation and explain why you have chosen that particular method.

Communication can also be categorised in the following ways.

- **Urgent** – this is information which needs to be passed on as a priority. In the public services, urgent information can literally mean life or death. Examples of this include 999 calls to an emergency service, or a report of child abuse which needs to be acted upon by social services.

- **Non-urgent** – this is information with no strict deadline.

- **Difficult** – lots of information in the public services can be difficult to communicate, either because it is very complex or distressing. You will need to choose a suitable style of communication for this sort of information, such as face-to-face.

- **Routine** – much of the communication in the public services is routine. This could include communicating information about shift patterns, ordering and maintaining equipment, writing incident reports and circulating minutes of meetings.

Writing skills

The ability to write is needed in most jobs, including the public services. The quality of your writing is very important, particularly if your written work could be read by an internal or external customer. The things you write reflect on your organisation and they must be written in a way that is appropriate to the situation.

The amount of written work undertaken in the public services varies. As a general rule, the higher your rank or position, the more writing you will do. However, there are some services where reports are more critical than others. For example, in the NHS, patient treatment depends on accurate written medical notes, and health visitors are required to keep comprehensive records on children under five years old. In the Police Service, reports may even form the basis of court cases.

Interpreting written information

The public services need their staff to be able to read and understand written information to an acceptable standard. For example, a social worker will be expected to have high reading ability because a substantial part of their role involves reading a large amount of written material.

You are also likely to come across a lot of written data in the public services and you will be expected to use this data to make appropriate decisions. For example, if you were a local authority officer you might have to understand the data from surveys of residents before deciding which services should be provided in their local area.

Because this is such an important skill, interpreting and drawing conclusions from written information is a major part of the interview and selection process for most public services. If you want to work for a service you will need to develop this skill.

Taking it further

Can you think of any other services where reports are extremely important to the service users? Work in small groups to identify two services where writing accurate reports is essential.

Did you know?

There are often rules that you must follow regarding the format of written documents. This is so that the public service has a standard written style. Sometimes, services will even have templates for written communication.

Activity 2.6   Understanding written information

Read the written account below.

An accident occurred on the M1 motorway between junctions 28 and 29 southbound at 2pm. The driver of a Vauxhall Astra was seen to pull into the middle lane without indicating, forcing another car to veer into the central reservation. One person suffered a broken arm and was taken to hospital before the police arrived.

Now answer these questions, using the answers 'true', 'false' or 'impossible to say'.

1 The accident was on the M1 motorway on the carriageway that leads to London.

2 The driver of the Vauxhall Astra was injured in the crash.

3 The central reservation was responsible for the accident.

4 The police did not give first aid at the scene.

5 The accident happened at 1400 hours.

▶ Appropriateness of communication style

It is important to match the right style of communication to the right situation. If urgent information needs to be communicated, you are unlikely to do this in a letter. However, if the information is less urgent, it may be best given in writing. For example, if there has been a recent crime wave in an area, then circulating informative leaflets about how to avoid becoming a victim of theft might be a good approach.

▶ Teamwork

The public services use teamwork in their day-to-day activities and work collaboratively with other public services. The characteristics of effective teams are outlined below.

Clearly defined team roles

The main aim of teamwork is to complete the tasks the team was initially set up to complete. For the Police Service, this task might be crime reduction. For HM Coastguard, it might be conducting a successful rescue.

A team cannot operate effectively to complete their tasks if the people in the team do not know what their responsibilities are. A good team has clearly defined roles, with each team member knowing exactly what their role is and how it fits in with the roles of the other team members.

Why do you think teamwork is so important in the public services?

This also applies when the public services work together. For example, at the scene of a traffic incident:

- the Police Service would apply a cordon and redirect traffic
- the Fire and Rescue Service would extract individuals from the scene and make the scene safe if chemicals such as petrol had been spilled
- the Ambulance Service would stabilise casualties at the scene and transport them to hospitals for further treatment.

What would happen if each team did not know its responsibilities?

Activity 2.7 — Different types of team

Working in pairs, carry out some research to create a poster which shows five or six different types of teams that work in the public services, e.g. shift, watch, regiment, etc. Give a brief description of each team you identify and state which service you are most likely to find it in.

Respecting, understanding and being aware of differences

Teamwork requires you to respect your fellow team members and their skills. Not everyone on a team has the same background or abilities, but they do not need to. Each person brings something to the team, making the team stronger and more effective than each individual would be on their own. These differences can include cultural knowledge and language skills.

Showing fairness and consideration

It is important to show fairness and consideration to your fellow team members. You may be working in a very tense situation, and individuals under pressure can sometimes find it challenging to get along. This means that it is vital to take care of each other and understand how difficult everyone's jobs are.

▶ Dealing with and managing change

Dealing with or managing change is something that the public services often have to do in their day-to-day jobs. This is because they often work in fast-changing or unpredictable situations, and they have to be able to adapt when the situation they are in changes. For example, in a major incident, any additional unforeseen circumstances can require an immediate change in approach.

Most public services are also directly affected by changes of government. This means that people who work in the public services need to be able to deal with or manage change. For example, at the time of publication, there is a huge amount of change affecting the public services. The country has less money to spend on both uniformed and non-uniformed services, and senior managers have to find different ways of working in order to save money. Everyone in the public sector has a responsibility to help manage these changes.

Remember

If you are fair and considerate with others, they are more likely to be fair and considerate with you. This makes your working life easier.

Contingency measures

'Contingency measures' is a professional way of saying 'plan B'. The nature of public service work means that, no matter how well you plan for an event, something is likely to change or go wrong. A good team can adapt what it is doing at very short notice to match the situation. This may involve having several different plans.

Agreeing, setting and monitoring achievement

Communication skills

It is important to have standards in place for communications in the public services because this ensures that communications from a service all sound professional and use a similar style. For more information about communication skills, see pages 48–54.

Punctuality

It is important to be on time and avoid being late. You must always make sure you have given yourself enough time, allowing for unforeseen circumstances that might delay you. Being punctual is a basic skill that everyone should try to maintain, particularly if you are a public service employee. In the public services, you are expected to be efficient and polite, and being late can be considered very rude. In some services, failing to arrive on time could endanger lives and property.

Personal presentation

Your personal presentation says a lot about you as a person or potential employee. We judge people by the way they look, dress and speak. For example, would you want a police officer to come and assist you if he or she was scruffy and wearing a dirty uniform? You would probably think they did not take their job seriously and that they might not be the best person to deal with your problem.

The public services want to ensure that the appearance of their employees creates a positive first impression on the public. A neat uniform can be key to showing pride in your work. For example, having polished shoes, an ironed shirt and pressed trousers shows that you are proud of your job and your position in society.

Behaviour towards others

Your behaviour, or the way you speak to and interact with people, is a key factor in how well you will be able to communicate with them. If your behaviour is inappropriate, the public may not trust you. Even worse, they may feel that the service they have received is not professional and they may feel let down by the public service you represent. This can cause problems for the public service as a whole: a service can have its reputation damaged by a few poor employees.

Health and safety

The purpose of health and safety is to stop you getting hurt at work or being made ill as a result of the work you do. All workers have the right to work in places where the risks of injury, ill-health or accident are minimised. This is particularly important for many public service workers who may find themselves in hazardous situations as part of their daily job.

Did you know?

Punctuality is extremely important to the emergency services. If they do not respond promptly to a 999 call lives can be lost. Ambulance trusts in England must respond to 75% of life-threatening situations within 8 minutes.

Did you know?

Risks can be present in any public sector job, not just in the armed or emergency services. In 2012–13, there were over 60,000 physical assaults against NHS staff in England.

Remember

Your own conduct and behaviour need to be extremely good. When you work in a public service, your behaviour reflects on the service as a whole.

Case study

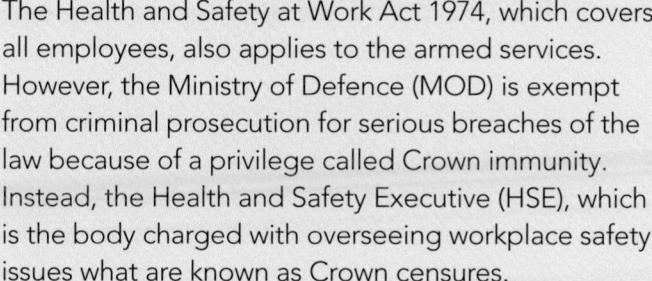

The Health and Safety at Work Act 1974, which covers all employees, also applies to the armed services. However, the Ministry of Defence (MOD) is exempt from criminal prosecution for serious breaches of the law because of a privilege called Crown immunity. Instead, the Health and Safety Executive (HSE), which is the body charged with overseeing workplace safety, issues what are known as Crown censures.

In July 2013, three Army Reserve soldiers died in the Brecon Beacons in Wales. They were taking part in an SAS selection training exercise when they collapsed on a hike in very high temperatures.

In September 2011, a 21-year-old Army Fusilier died at a shooting range in Kent. He was taking part in a live firing exercise.

1 Do you think the MOD should be exempt from prosecution?

2 What could the armed services do to minimise the risks of incidents such as the ones in the case study?

3 Can you identify the difficulties the armed services would face if they were subject to HSE prosecution?

4 Do you know employees' health and safety responsibilities? Name as many as you can.

Quality of work

If you join a public service, you are expected to uphold that service's standards and deliver high-quality work. The public pays the public services, so they have a right to expect their public servants to provide them with excellent service.

Consistency of customer service

It is important for the public services to deliver consistent customer service. If quality is not consistent, the service's reputation may be damaged and people may not want to use the service. In addition, if some customers are seen to be treated differently, accusations of favouritism or discrimination could be levelled at the service.

▮▶ Working to an agreed common goal

Cooperation is very important in teams. It means working together to achieve a common goal and supporting each other in achieving that goal – even when some team members have very different viewpoints. Team members have to cooperate with each other in order to complete a task, particularly if someone's life depends on it.

▮▶ Occupational skills

There are lots of different skills which you will need to develop which are related to the type of job or occupation you plan to do in the future and the specific public service you might want to join. Examples of this include dealing with conflict and dealing with the public.

Dealing with conflict

Every day the public services have to deal with people who are traumatised, frightened or aggressive. This can often lead to conflict. Think about the police arriving on the scene after a traffic accident, when the people involved may be in a dispute over who was at fault. The officers must deal with the dispute quickly to ensure it does not escalate into violence. People may be injured further or evidence lost, so it is important to deal with the conflict quickly. This is often done by using listening and speaking techniques designed to calm the situation.

Discussion

Do you think it is important that all customers receive the same quality of service?

Remember

It is important that you do not let your personal feelings towards other team members get in the way of the job that needs to be done. A good team leader can help prevent this and ensure that everyone pulls in the same direction.

Similarly, when social services have to conduct home visits to assess the welfare of children, they may find themselves in a very hostile or tense environment. They need special skills to do their job so they can avoid making the situation worse for the family and children involved.

Activity 2.8 — Dealing with conflict

Most of us encounter conflict at some point in our personal and professional lives. Think of a situation where you have experienced conflict and consider the questions below.

- What was your part in creating the conflict?
- How did you behave during the conflict?
- How did you help to resolve the conflict?
- What would you do differently next time?

Dealing with the public

Most people who work in the public sector come into contact with the public on a daily basis. It is important to use all the skills we have identified in this section to serve the public well.

▌▶ Personal and interpersonal skills

Figure 2.2 shows some of the key interpersonal skills you will need to work effectively in the public sector. These skills will all fit together, like the pieces in a jigsaw, to make you an effective member of the public services.

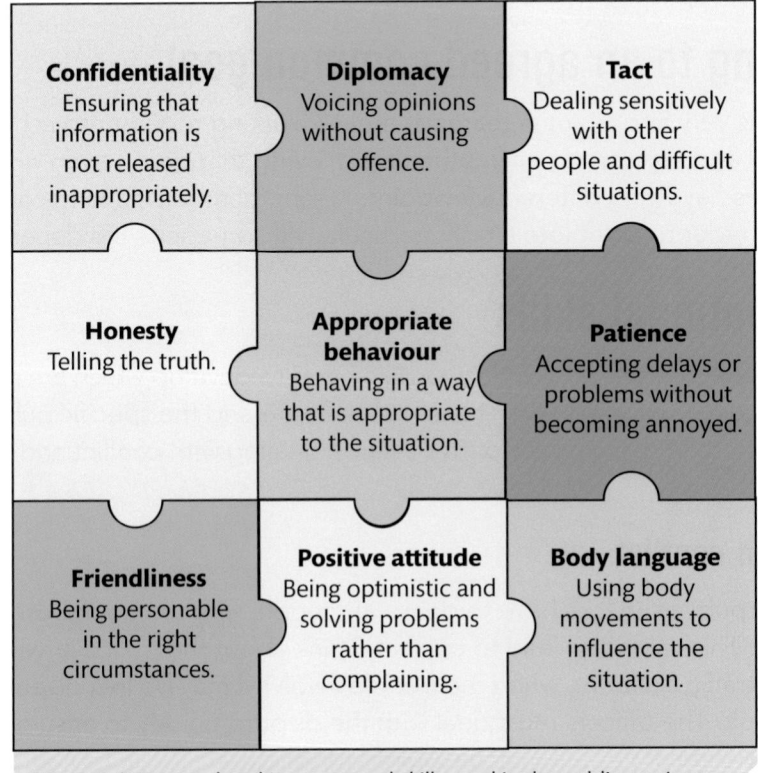

Figure 2.2: Personal and interpersonal skills used in the public services.

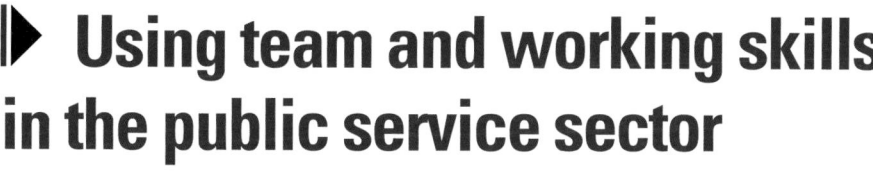

Assessment activity 2.1 · *English*

You work for a large public sector employer. They have asked you to write a report on the improvements they can make when working with customers. You need to carry out some research into a wide range of public services and compare the customer service they offer.

Investigate the internal and external customers of two contrasting public services and review how these services meet the needs of their customers.

Consider the working skills used by two contrasting public services and discuss how those skills are used to meet customer needs.

Tip

- Choose to research two contrasting public services from different groups, such as one armed service and one service from the voluntary sector.

Learning aim B   **TOPIC**   **B.1**

Using team and working skills in the public service sector

Introduction

Knowing the skills that public sector workers need is one thing, but being able to demonstrate them is another. Have you ever been in a situation where you have needed some of the skills we have been discussing? Think about the service you are most interested in. What skills would you need to demonstrate to be a good team member in this service?

Applying working skills through teamwork

Often you will find that, in order to apply your teamwork skills, you need to actively take part in tasks which are designed to get you and your colleagues working together. These activities are called teambuilding activities and different types of teambuilding activities include:

- **icebreakers** and improving communication
- eliminating **stereotypes** and labelling
- building **interdependence** and trust
- problem solving.

Key terms

Icebreakers – activities which help introduce people and allow them to get to know each other.

Stereotypes – widely held views which present an oversimplified or generalised opinion.

Interdependence – relying on others and having them rely on you.

Before you decide to work on teambuilding, you need to know if your team has any particular problems that need to be improved. Consider the questions below.

- Are there conflicts between certain team members that are creating divisions within the team?
- Do team members need to get to know one another?
- Do some members focus on their own success, and harm the group as a result?
- Does poor communication slow your group's progress?
- Do people need to learn how to work together, instead of individually?

Do you think that any of these problems apply to a team you are part of? How could you choose a teambuilding activity to overcome these problems?

Activity 2.9   Survival scenario

This exercise forces your group to communicate and agree, in order to ensure their 'survival'.

You are part of a group of four people in a boat which has just been seriously damaged and will sink in 10 minutes. There is a desert island nearby and there is room on the lifeboat for each person, plus 12 items you will need to survive on the island. You can choose from the following:

• first aid kit	• matches	• hat
• food	• seeds	• toilet roll
• binoculars	• flares	• compass
• tent	• knife	• metal bowl
• blankets	• whistle	• smartphone
• fishing rod	• pen	• laptop
• axe	• hooks	• watch
• mirror	• torch	• guitar
• survival manual	• rope	• radio.
• empty plastic bottle	• sun cream	

1 Consider which 12 items you will take and why. Everyone must agree before any one item can be put into the lifeboat.

2 Consider what you will use each item for.

3 List your top five survival priorities when you reach the island.

Take it further

Can you think of any teambuilding activities of your own? Look online to see the range of teambuilding activities available. Consider how you could adapt them to help your class or group improve their teamwork.

Other useful teambuilding activities include:

- the great egg drop – your team designs and builds a container to protect an egg from an eight foot drop
- blind stroll or blind obstacle course – three members of your team are blindfolded and you must guide them around a small obstacle course.

▶ Applying working skills

There are many situations in the public services where effective working skills will be essential. Table 2.1 shows some examples.

Table 2.1: Examples of situations where teamworking is essential in the public services.

Service	Situation where teamworking is essential
Emergency services	Responding to a road traffic incident.
Armed services	Engaging in armed conflict or peacekeeping activities.
Local authority	Coordinating repairs to social housing and responding to customer complaints.
Central government	Developing new laws in parliament.
Voluntary services	Providing aid to areas which have experienced natural disasters such as flooding or supporting large outdoor events such as festivals.

Activity 2.10   Teamworking

Choose a teambuilding exercise and lead the rest of the group through the exercise. How did they do? How useful do you think this exercise would be in the service you would like to join?

TOPIC   B.2

▶ Reviewing performance of application of working skills through teamwork

Introduction

Have you ever thought about what your strengths are or made an action plan to improve a skill? Members of the public services have to review their job performance regularly and take action to improve their weaknesses. List your strengths and weaknesses. How can you improve your skills?

▶ Identifying strengths and areas for improvement

You need to be able to look at your personal skills and identify your own strengths and areas for improvement if you are going to improve your performance.

Some common strengths include:

- hard working
- good communication skills
- gets on well with others
- listens and understands.

Link

See Figure 2.2 on page 58 for examples of the personal, interpersonal and communication skills you might need to use when working in the public services.

Some common weaknesses or areas for improvement include:

- lack of assertiveness
- too aggressive
- shy
- lack of motivation.

Each activity you undertake in the public services may require skills which are specific to the activity, such as using particular equipment, as well as more non-specific skills, such as interpersonal and communication skills.

Key term

SWOT analysis – a self-analysis technique in which you consider the Strengths, Weaknesses, Opportunities and Threats of a project or yourself.

▶ Carrying out self-analysis

There are many different ways of carrying out self-analysis, such as **SWOT analysis**, watching a video of your own performance or completing a self-evaluation checklist.

Recording your performance

If you are doing a practical task, one of the best ways of analysing your performance is to video the task and then watch the video to see what you could improve. This method is also good for looking at team activities, as you will be able to see more clearly where things might be going wrong.

SWOT analysis

SWOT stands for **S**trengths, **W**eaknesses, **O**pportunities and **T**hreats. SWOT analysis is a way of looking at yourself from several different angles and using your findings to make a decision or draw conclusions.

Activity 2.11   SWOT analysis

India has completed her BTEC First Award in Public Services and needs to decide whether to apply to join a service, continue her studies or do something completely different. She has drawn up the following SWOT analysis.

India's SWOT analysis

Strengths	Opportunities
• Likes learning • Prepared to undergo further training • Has supportive family • Confident • Good communication skills • Good health • No ties or commitments	• Join the Army straight away • Do an IT course • Take a year out to travel • Work in a civilian job to get some experience
Weaknesses	**Threats**
• Not old enough for the Police Service • Lack of work experience • Lack of life experience • Not physically fit	• May be other candidates with more experience • May regret joining a service too young

---

1 Based on India's SWOT analysis, what do you think she should do?
2 Do you think there are any other threats or opportunities that India has not considered?
3 Draw up a SWOT analysis for yourself.

Skills audit

A skills audit is another way of assessing your suitability for a chosen career. This is a way of measuring and recording your skills and abilities and comparing them to the skills needed for a certain job. There are many methods of evaluating your skills and abilities, both on the internet and in self-development books.

Skills audits usually cover core skills used in the public services, such as:

* confidence, including your ability to cope with new situations or talk to people you have not met before
* communication skills, including your vocabulary and your body language
* teamworking skills, including your ability to work with others, take orders and participate positively in discussions
* interpersonal skills, including your diplomacy, fairness and sensitivity to the feelings of others
* conflict management skills, including your ability to keep calm, to calm others and to resolve conflict situations.

Improvement plan

An improvement plan or action plan will help you turn areas of weakness into strengths. It will also help you to monitor the process of self-improvement so that you know how far you have progressed towards your goals. For example, if your area of weakness is a failure to resolve conflict, then your objective would be to become effective in that skill. The way of achieving this could include going on training courses and getting more experience in conflict resolution situations.

When creating a personal development action plan, you should:

* identify the problem
* set an objective (or objectives) to achieve
* detail how you intend to meet your objectives
* describe the support you need from others
* list any resources you might need access to
* set dates for review or completion.

You may be familiar with many of these points from your own school or college's tutorial procedure.

Activity 2.12   Improvement plans

Tom is taking a BTEC First in Public Services at his local college. He has identified some weaknesses which he would like to improve. Figure 2.3 is a copy of his improvement plan.

Using Tom's improvement plan as a template, complete the following tasks.

1 Identify something you want to achieve, such as joining a service, getting fit or improving your assignment grades.

2 Draw up an action plan, based on Tom's, which will help you to achieve your goals.

Tom's personal improvement plan

Area(s) for development

My interpersonal communication skills are weak and I find myself not understanding situations because I don't have the confidence to ask what is going on. This will be a disadvantage if I decide to join the Police Service.

Targets to achieve

1. To improve my understanding of body language.
2. To become more aware of my own body language.
3. To develop the confidence to ask for help in situations if I don't understand what is going on.
4. To find out what interpersonal skills the police require in a potential recruit.

Actions required by me

1. Ask a close friend to monitor my body language to see if I am communicating in a friendly manner.
2. Make a diary of body language that I see and use a good quality body language book to see what it means.
3. Consider going on a course on interpersonal communication to improve my skills and confidence.
4. Research the interpersonal skills needed by the police.

Actions required by others

1. Friends and family to help me by monitoring my actions and giving me their advice.

Resources

- College prospectus
- Police application information
- Good quality body language book

Dates for review

I will review the situation every two weeks to see the progress I have made and change the action plan if needed:
- 30th January • 15th February • 1st March • 15th March.

Date for completion

By 15th March I should have achieved my targets completely.

Figure 2.3: An example of an improvement plan.

Assessment activity 2.2 — *English*

To show you can work as part of a team, you will take part in two teamwork activities:

1 simulated communications exercise using radios or non-verbal communications

2 fire safety campaign designed to prevent young people making hoax calls to the Fire and Rescue Service.

You need to play a different role in each scenario and act positively as a member of the team, demonstrating your teamwork skills. At the end, you need to consider your own performance as part of the team, thinking about what your strengths were and what you can do to develop an action plan to overcome your weaknesses.

Tips

- Try to play an active part in the simulation to show your effective teamwork skills.
- Be honest about what went well and what you need to do to improve.

WorkSpace

▶ Charlie Thompson

Social worker

I am a social worker with a large local authority. My job can sometimes be very difficult – because social workers are usually only needed when things are not going well, you often only see the negative side of family life. You have to help the individuals and families involved without being judgemental.

My role depends almost entirely on my communication skills. I need to be able to speak with people of all ages and backgrounds, including people who speak English as a second language, so making sure that people understand me can be a challenge. My working day can involve speaking with very young children, frightened children and distressed parents who feel unable to cope, as well as a range of other professionals including the police and teachers.

I have to write a lot of reports, which means that my written communication has to be as good as my verbal communication. If my reports are misunderstood, it could have terrible consequences for families and children at risk.

The best part of my job is helping families in crisis and seeing them come through it. Afterwards, you often see that families are better able to cope, and the children perform better at school and are much happier. You feel like you are able to make a real difference to the families and children who need it most.

Think about it

1 Why is excellent written and verbal communication required for the role of social worker?

2 Have you considered social work as a career? What are your reasons?

3 What things have you learned in this unit that will help you to work productively in a public sector role like this?

Introduction

This unit will inform you about the public service jobs that are available and how to prepare yourself for employment. There are many uniformed public service jobs, but there are even more public service jobs which are not uniformed. The lack of a uniform does not mean that these roles are any less important to the public – they just operate in a different way.

You will have the opportunity to explore the terms and conditions of employment in the public services. How many days' holiday can you expect? Where will you work? What will your shift patterns be? These factors might influence your choice of public service and so it is very important to consider them from the start.

You will also look in detail at the application and selection procedures for the public services. When you have completed this unit, you should be in a good position to start applying for jobs.

Assessment: This unit will be assessed through a series of assignments set by your tutor/teacher.

Learning aims

In this unit you will:

A understand employment roles and conditions of service in the public services

B explore employment in the public services.

"I do voluntary work in my spare time, but I wasn't really sure which service I would like to join. This unit gave me a lot to think about in terms of comparing future career options and helping me develop the skills I will need to get through the application process.

Tanya, *14-year-old St John Ambulance volunteer*

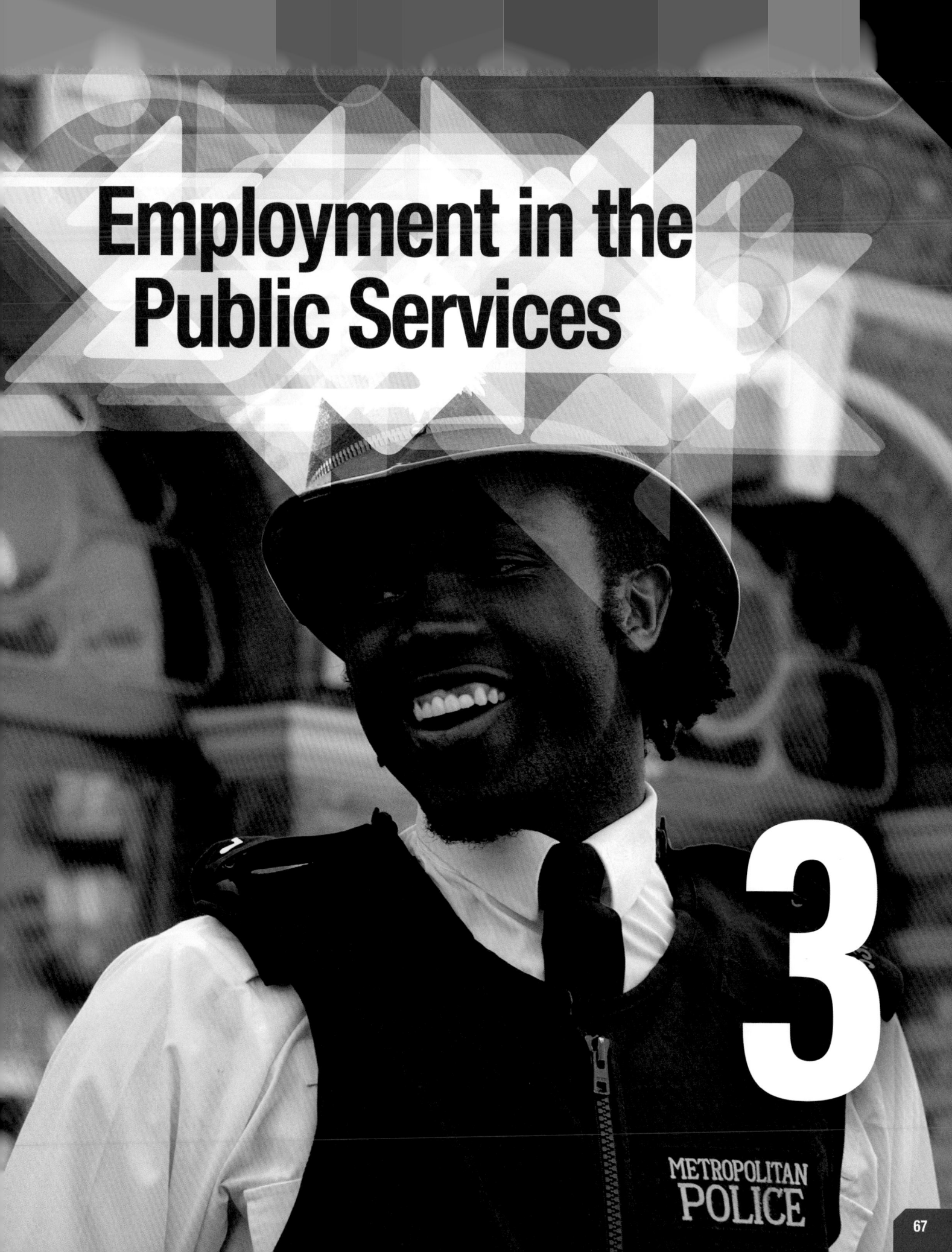

Employment in the Public Services

BTEC
Assessment Zone

This table shows you what you must do in order to achieve a **Pass**, **Merit** or **Distinction** grade, and where you can find activities to help you.

Assessment criteria			
Level 1	**Level 2 Pass**	**Level 2 Merit**	**Level 2 Distinction**
Learning aim A: Understand employment roles and conditions of service in the public services			
1A.1 English Outline the range of work undertaken by two contrasting public services.	**2A.P1** English Describe, using relevant examples, the range of work undertaken by three contrasting public services. **See Assessment activity 3.1, page 85**	**2A.M1** Compare the range of work undertaken by three contrasting public services. **See Assessment activity 3.1, page 85**	**2A.D1** Evaluate the advantages and disadvantages of employment in three contrasting public services. **See Assessment activity 3.1, page 85**
1A.2 English Identify job roles available in two contrasting public services.	**2A.P2** English Explain the requirements for job roles available in three contrasting public services. **See Assessment activity 3.1, page 85**	**2A.M2** Compare the requirements for job roles available in three contrasting public services. **See Assessment activity 3.1, page 85**	
Learning aim B: Explore employment in the public services			
1B.3 Identify the application and selection process for a public service job.	**2B.P3** Describe the application and selection process for two public service jobs from contrasting public services. **See Assessment activity 3.2, page 98**	**2B.M3** Compare the application and selection process for two public service jobs, from contrasting public services. **See Assessment activity 3.2, page 98**	**2B.D2** Analyse the application and selection process for two public service jobs, from contrasting public services. **See Assessment activity 3.2, page 98**
1B.4 English Use job-searching techniques to find two suitable job opportunities in the public service sector from given sources of information.	**2B.P4** English Use job-searching techniques to find two suitable job opportunities in the public service sector from researched sources of information. **See Assessment activity 3.2, page 98**	**2B.M4** English Compare the suitability for self of two selected job opportunities in public services, identifying areas for improvement of own skills. **See Assessment activity 3.2, page 98**	**2B.D3** English Evaluate the suitability of self for two selected job opportunities in public services, recommending the most suitable option. **See Assessment activity 3.2, page 98**
1B.5 English Complete a written application for a selected vacancy using appropriate language and tone.	**2B.P5** English Produce a structured written application for a selected vacancy using appropriate language and tone. **See Assessment activity 3.2, page 98**	**2B.M5** English Produce a structured and detailed written application, using appropriate language and tone, which meets the requirements of a suitable vacancy . **See Assessment activity 3.2, page 98**	**2B.D4** English Produce a well-organised presentation of a written application, which is fit for purpose and fully meets the requirements of the selected vacancy. **See Assessment activity 3.2, page 98**

English Opportunity to practise English skills

How you will be assessed

This unit will be assessed by a series of assignments set by your tutor. You will need to explore the range of job roles in the public services and find out about the requirements of these roles.

You will also investigate job opportunities, assess your own suitability for different roles, and complete an application for a public service role of your choice.

Your assignment could be in the form of:

- a booklet
- an information pack
- an exhibition
- a completed application form.

POLICE

▶ The work undertaken by the public services

Introduction

Different public service organisations employ people in very different roles while still working effectively together. You explored many of these organisations in Unit 1, but here you will look at the types of roles available and their working conditions. What do you know about the variety of roles you could do in each service? Do you think that some jobs may be more difficult to get than other jobs?

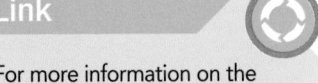

Link

For more information on the groups of public services see Unit 1, Topic A.1 (pages 4–16).

The public service sector is broadly divided up into particular groups of public service jobs. Table 3.1 lists these groups.

Table 3.1: Groups of public service.

Public service	Description
Emergency services	• Often called 'blue light' services because of the flashing lights on their vehicles. They are the services you would get if you dialled 999. • Include the Police Service, the Fire and Rescue Service and the Ambulance Service.
Armed services	• Deployed to conflict situations and peacekeeping operations, and support the emergency services in situations such as terrorist incidents and severe weather events. • Include the British Army, the Royal Air Force and the Royal Navy.
Local authorities	• Provide local services such as refuse collection, children's services, social services and social housing. • Include organisations such as county councils, district councils and city councils.
Central government	• Public services that are provided directly through a government ministry, such as the Prison Service and Her Majesty's Revenue and Customs. • Includes the civil service which supports our Members of Parliament.
Voluntary or third sector	• Fills a gap in the public services which is not filled by either the public sector or the private sector. • Includes organisations such as the British Red Cross, St John Ambulance and other charities.

These groups perform a wide range of tasks and undertake different types of work. Individuals who work in the public services are often required to do jobs which can change from minute to minute in response to rapidly changing circumstances.

All of the services need specific sets of skills. They train you in these after you have been accepted as a recruit. For example, the Royal Navy will teach you shipboard firefighting skills, the Prison Service will teach you restraint techniques and the Ambulance Service will train you in the administration of medication. You are not expected to have these skills already – they are skills you gain on the job.

▶ Emergency services

The emergency services such as the police, fire and ambulance services carry out a wide range of tasks. Generally, these can be classed as routine, non-routine, community and administrative tasks, as well as roles at major incidents.

Routine activities

Routine activities are what people in the emergency services do on a day-to-day basis. Depending on the service, it may include activities such as:

- preventing and investigating crime
- treating injuries or sudden illness and transporting people to hospital
- responding to fires
- reassuring the community and educating the public about staying safe.

Non-routine activities

These are activities which do not happen every day. They are special or unusual duties. They make up a small minority of what the emergency services do in an ordinary day or week, and can include activities such as:

- dealing with terrorist incidents
- emergency flood response.

Case study

On 7 July 2005, London was the subject of a terrorist attack which targeted its transport network, including the London Underground and London Buses. The attack killed 52 people and injured more than 770, and was planned to occur during the rush hour to cause maximum casualties.

Three separate bombs went off around 8.50 a.m. on Underground trains near Liverpool Street station, Edgware Road station and between King's Cross and Russell Square stations. An hour later, a bomb exploded on a double-decker bus in Tavistock Square. These bombings were carried out by four separate suicide bombers.

1 Why is this incident called a non-routine activity?

2 How can the emergency services prepare for non-routine activities such as this?

3 How should the services work together to ensure a non-routine incident such as this can be dealt with quickly and effectively?

Roles at major incidents

Responding to major incidents is a responsibility of all three primary emergency services. A major incident is an event in which special arrangements to respond to an incident have to be put in place by one or more services. Major incidents include terrorist attacks, flooding, earthquakes, nuclear incidents, major road traffic collisions and large-scale public order situations.

The roles of the emergency services at the scene of a major incident will depend on the type of incident and the service in question, but usually the following actions are taken.

- The scene of the incident is maintained so that evidence of any crime can be collected and preserved.
- Security cordons are set up so that only authorised people can enter, ensuring that no other people are put at risk and the work of the services is not hindered by bystanders.
- Fires and accidents are dealt with.
- Search and rescue operations are carried out.
- Lives are saved and further damage to property is prevented.
- Medical care and transportation to hospital are provided.
- The release of information to the media and the public is controlled.

Did you know?

The Civil Contingencies Act 2004 defines a major incident or emergency as an event or situation which threatens death, injury, damage to property or the environment, or war or terrorism.

Just checking

1 What is a major incident?
2 List three types of major incident.
3 Identify three things that need to happen at the scene of a major incident.

Community work

The emergency services also do a lot of community work, particularly in schools to educate young people about personal safety, drugs and fire safety. Some services also have youth schemes such as firefighter or police cadet schemes.

Administrative work

Much of the work of the emergency services involves paperwork. This includes arrest reports, reports on fires, patient records, and so on. This paperwork has to be accurate and clear as it may be used as evidence in court or to inform hospital treatment.

Remember

The public services have to complete a lot of paperwork and it needs to be done clearly and accurately. This is why you need very good English skills. If your writing, reading, spelling or punctuation need to be improved, do this before you apply for a public service.

Work with other public services

The emergency services have to work very closely with each other, but also very closely with other services such as the local authority, the courts and sometimes the armed services. This is particularly the case during a major incident.

▶ Armed services

The armed services are the Royal Air Force (RAF), the Royal Navy and the British Army, plus their reserve forces. They do a wide range of work in this country and overseas.

Routine activities

Everyday activities for the armed services can range from simple tasks such as maintaining equipment to high publicity events such as the changing of the guard. Some of the most common routine activities include:

- active service in conflict situations
- peacekeeping missions
- military exercises and training
- security patrols and guard duty
- maintaining kit and equipment
- ceremonial duties.

Non-routine activities

As with emergency services, non-routine activities are those outside the armed services' normal range of work. This can include things such as escorting state funerals or assisting at other state occasions, such as the funeral of the former Prime Minister, Margaret Thatcher. During the funeral procession, her coffin rested on a gun carriage drawn by the King's Troop Royal Horse Artillery and the route was lined by military personnel from all three services. Bands from the Scots Guards and the Welsh Guards of the Household Division, the Royal Marines and the RAF played along the route of the procession.

Humanitarian work

The armed services also do a great deal of humanitarian work. For example, in Kenya, the British Army operates the International Mine Action Training Centre. The centre was set up to reduce the suffering caused by land mines and provide vital mine action training. In 2005, the armed services sent 500,000 ration packs to New Orleans after the disaster of Hurricane Katrina.

Military assistance to the civil community

The armed services are sometimes called upon to assist the emergency services and local authorities in times of disaster or emergency. In recent years, this includes flood defence and rescue and public service strikes. For example, in 2002, the armed services covered firefighting duties during a series of fire brigade strikes.

Administrative work

Like other public services, the armed services have to do a lot of administrative work. Running three services with over 200,000 employees does not happen without excellent administrative support and logistics provision.

Work with other public services

The armed services work closely with each other on training and exercises and also with the military organisations of our allies. This means that British troops sometimes train alongside troops from other nations. This is assisted by the Connected Forces Initiative led by the North Atlantic Treaty Organization (NATO).

Take it further

Ceremonial duties include Changing the Guard and Trooping the Colour. Do some research and find out what each of these ceremonies is used for and why it is important.

Did you know?

State and ceremonial funerals are very expensive. Margaret Thatcher's funeral is thought to have cost £1.2 million. This included costs for policing and security, as well as Ambulance Service costs. 4,000 police officers were on duty in central London on that day, and 700 military personnel were involved in the event.

Link

See the case study in Unit 1 (page 5) for an example of how the armed services supported the emergency services during the December 2013 floods.

Take it further

Use NATO's website to do some independent research on the Connected Forces Initiative. What is the initiative designed to do? How will it help troops from different NATO countries work together more effectively?

▶ Local authorities

Local authorities are made up of local government organisations such as county councils and district councils. They deliver a wide range of services to their local communities.

Routine activities

Routine day-to-day activity for a local authority is very large and complex. Local authorities are arguably the public service with the widest range of services, touching the lives of the most citizens, so working with the public is their key task. Some of their routine activities include:

- collecting and recycling waste
- managing libraries, museums and cultural services
- providing education and child protection services
- managing and allocating social housing
- providing leisure and sports facilities
- providing services for vulnerable adults and families.

Non-routine activities

For a local authority, non-routine activities can include any number of things, such as planning for major sporting events or working with the emergency services to deal with flooding or other environmental damage.

Administrative work

Local authorities have to do significant volumes of administration in order to ensure that those in most need receive the services they require. Councils can deliver hundreds of different services to local populations of several hundred thousand people. This could not happen without investment in systems and personnel to ensure that accurate records are kept and documentation is completed.

Work with other public services

Local authorities have to work closely with all three main emergency services to ensure that a proper response to any major incident is conducted.

Did you know?

Over 150 councils across the UK were involved in the 2012 Olympic torch relay, which cost over £6 million. This puts the average cost of hosting the Olympic torch at around £40,000 per local council.

Activity 3.1 Local authority services

Visit the website for your local authority and identify as many of the services they offer as you can. What do you think are the most important services they offer? Which services do you think are less important?

▶ Central government

Routine activities

Central government consists of government departments that manage or devolve the public services. They set the strategy and direction for the whole country, including the public sector.

Routine work for central government includes:

- administering government departments such as the Home Office
- reporting to ministers so the government is aware of key issues facing the services
- deciding and implementing public service strategy.

Non-routine activities

Activities that fall outside the central government's normal range of work include:

- dealing with threats to national security
- severe weather conditions
- major incidents affecting large areas of the country.

Administrative work

Administrative work makes up the majority of central government work because central government administers the remainder of the public sector. It sets the budgets and strategy for the services.

Liaising with other public services

Central government manages the public services. This means that liaison is largely confined to communication and guidance from central government to the services, and feedback on the impact of those decisions from the services to central government.

▶ The voluntary or third sector

The voluntary sector is made up of charities and organisations that use volunteers in place of permanent employees. They often offer services that neither the public nor private sectors offer. This could include providing emotional support for victims of crime or raising money to research treatments and cures for disease.

Routine activities

Routine activities vary considerably between charities, depending on why they exist and what they are trying to achieve. However, charities generally undertake the routine activities shown in Figure 3.1.

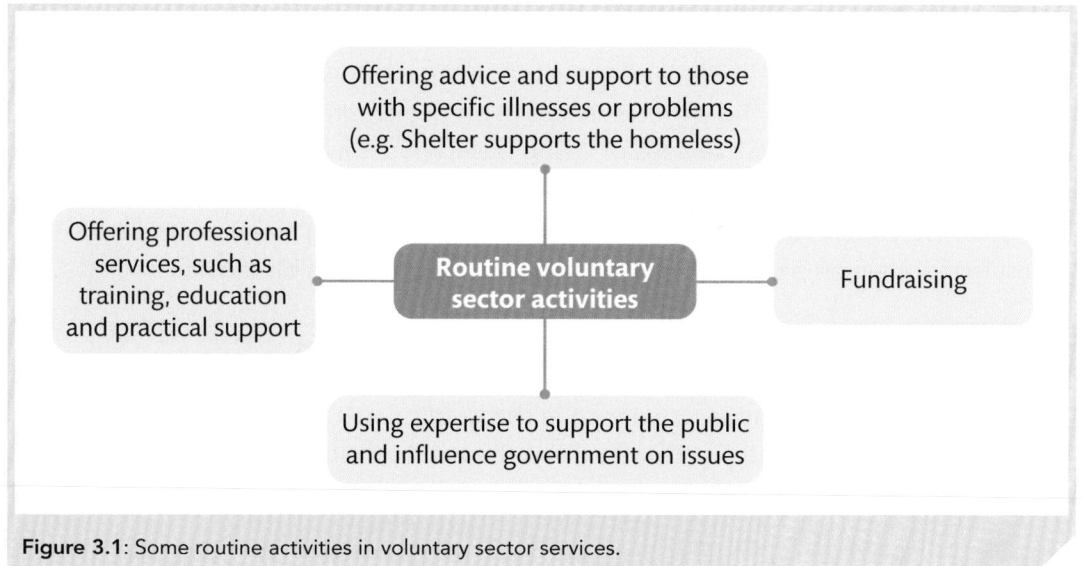

Figure 3.1: Some routine activities in voluntary sector services.

Did you know?

Central government holds a crisis committee in the event of a large-scale regional or national crisis. This is known as COBRA, after the room in which the committee meets (Cabinet Office Briefing Room A).

Discussion

Central government is made up of MPs and administrative staff called civil servants, who enable MPs to do their jobs. There are more than 420,000 civil servants in the UK. This compares with nearly 130,000 police officers. Do you think we need so many civil servants? Discuss your thoughts.

Administrative work

Administrative work is necessary to organise effective service delivery. However, most charities are very efficient with their administration costs, as they want to use their money to support people instead.

Work to support the public services

Some voluntary sector services work to support the public services in areas such as Victim Support, which offers advice and help to people who have been victims of crime. Voluntary services also include the many mental health and cancer charities which offer support to NHS patients.

> ### Take it further
>
> Many public service students actively raise money for charity either as individuals or as a class or group, or choose to volunteer for a charity. Have you and your colleagues raised any money recently? What good cause could you raise money for and what could you do to raise the money?

▶ Positive and negative aspects of working in the services

Working in the public services can look glamorous and exciting, especially on television. In reality, though, working in the public services is just like working in any other job – it has its advantages and its disadvantages.

Some positive aspects of working in a public service are outlined below.

- **Pride** – for many people working in the public sector, their job is a source of personal pride. They value what they do and are proud of giving service to the country. Taking pride in your job is important in the public services.
- **Respect** – many people give the public services and their employees a level of respect and admiration that they do not give to people in other professions. This is because they recognise the difficult and dangerous work that is undertaken and know that it requires dedication.
- **Travel opportunities** – the armed services in particular offer opportunities to spend extensive time travelling overseas or being based outside of the UK.
- **Personal and professional development** – the services are very good at developing people. They spend significant amounts of money on training and equipment to ensure that their employees can give the public the best possible service.

> ### Activity 3.2   Advantages of working in the public services
>
> There are many advantages to working in the public services. Can you think of any other advantages? Identify and write down the main advantages as you see them – consider things such as pay and working conditions as well.

There is a sense of pride associated with working in the armed services. Do you feel proud of the men and women who serve?

Some negative aspects of working in a public service are outlined below.

- **Risks to self** – working in many of the services comes with a risk of harm to yourself. This is because you may be putting yourself between the object or person causing the harm and the general public. It is not just members of the armed and emergency services who may be at risk of serious harm while on duty. Almost 60,000 NHS staff are assaulted each year while on duty.

- **Negative public perception** – some services can be perceived negatively by the public. If you work in a service which some of the population do not respect, they may be rude to you.

- **Unsociable shift patterns** – shift work is common in most public services, because services offered often need to be available 24 hours a day, 7 days a week, such as the emergency services. This means that some staff work at night or over Christmas. This can have a significant impact on your personal life.

- **Working away from home** – many services, such as the armed services, have to work away from home for extended periods of time. This can be difficult not just for the servicemen and women but also for their parents, spouses, children and other loved ones.

- **Stress** – public sector work is very stressful, whether the work is saving people's lives in emergencies or dealing with people as a local authority housing officer. The people you come into contact with will often be stressed, and it would be very easy for their distress to upset you. Research has shown that those who routinely deal with people in distress often experience higher levels of stress and burnout than other workers.

- **Dealing with difficult situations** – the public services are usually called in when something has gone wrong. They often deal with horrific events, including death and severe injuries, and dangerous situations. Not everyone could cope with this type of work.

 Did you know?

In 2012, research found that the average public sector worker takes 9.1 days a year in sick leave, compared to 5.7 days taken by the average private sector worker. The leading cause of public service leave is work-related stress.

 Discussion

Naval deployments can be up to 7 months long. How would you feel about being away from home for that length of time? How would your family cope? Discuss how you would approach these working conditions.

▶ Public service job opportunities

Introduction

There are many different types of job opportunity in the services. You will know about the most well-known jobs, such as police officer and firefighter, but there is a whole range of other operational and support roles available. Have you thought about the range of jobs in the service you want to join? Have you considered working in a support role rather than an operational role?

▶ Jobs in the armed services

The armed services employ nearly 170,000 trained personnel and around 65,000 civilian support workers, so there is a whole range of jobs in the armed services. The different types of role are shown in Figure 3.2.

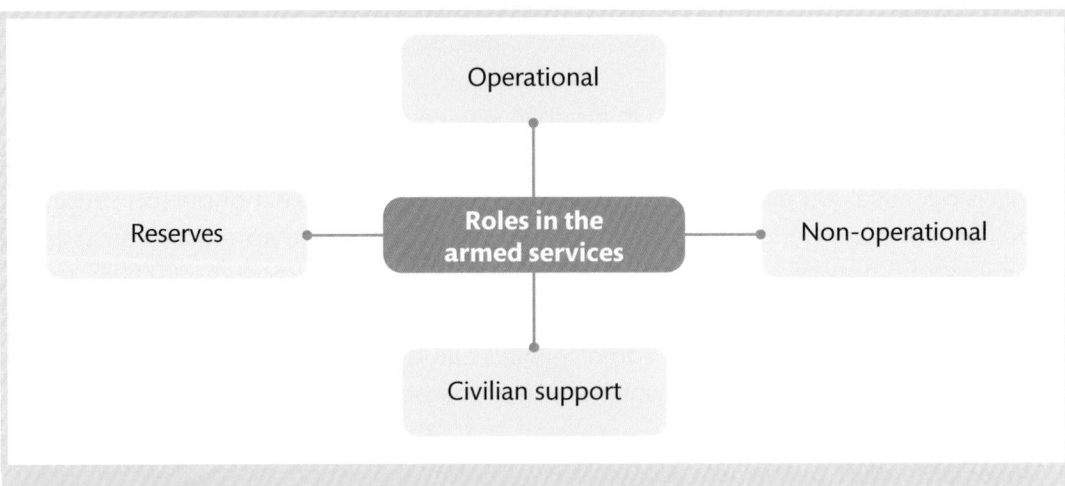

Figure 3.2: Different types of role in the armed services.

Operational roles

Operational roles in the armed services are those which have a direct impact on operational duties and missions. These include jobs such as:

- sailor
- Royal Marine
- RAF pilot
- air traffic controller
- paratrooper
- weapons handler.

Discussion

At the time of writing, the British Army does not allow women to serve in front line infantry units. However, other nations have opened up combat units to women. Why do you think there are restrictions on which units women can serve in? What are the perceived benefits of this to the British Army? Do you think this discrimination is justified on the basis of combat effectiveness or is it just down to old-fashioned values?

Role case study

British Army – infantry soldier

Infantry soldiers are at the front line of any combat situation. They are the ground troops who are involved in operations ranging from peacekeeping and disaster relief to active combat in war zones. There are no formal qualifications needed to join the infantry, but good English and maths skills are useful. The British Infantry is only open to men.

Entrance requirements

- Male
- 16–32 years of age
- No formal qualifications

Role case study

Royal Navy – mine warfare specialist

This is a highly specialised role, using mine-hunting sonar systems to detect naval mines and deploy remote vehicles to deal with them. This makes the seas safer for both military and civilian ships. There are no specific qualifications required for this role, though, as with all roles, good English, maths and teamworking skills are very useful. It is a very practical job – mine warfare specialists are often based aboard smaller ships and operate in all kinds of weather.

Entrance requirements

- 16–36 years of age
- No specific qualifications
- Commitment
- Enthusiasm
- Common sense
- Willingness to work in all weathers
- Good teamwork skills

Non-operational roles

Non-operational roles are those that do not routinely see front line combat. They include jobs such as:

- administrators
- medical personnel
- technical support.

Role case study

Royal Air Force – nursing officer

Nursing officers provide high quality medical care to RAF staff and other armed service personnel depending on the circumstances. The type of work can include nursing on a ward in a British hospital or field hospital overseas, treating injured servicemen and women who have been sent back to the UK or carrying out treatment onboard medical evacuation planes.

Entrance requirements

- Citizen of the UK or Republic of Ireland, or Commonwealth citizen since birth
- Professionally registered nurse (with a degree or diploma)
- GCSEs in English and maths at grade C
- Two years' nursing experience
- Registration with the Nursing and Midwifery Council

Civilian support

Civilian support in the armed services can take a number of forms, including human resources, finance, catering and cleaning. These jobs are filled by ordinary civilians who are security-cleared to work on military bases and with military colleagues where required.

Link

For more information about British military reserve forces, see Unit 1 (pages 9–10).

Voluntary

The armed service reserves are the volunteer support for all three armed services. They include the Royal Naval Reserves, the Army Reserves and the RAF Reserves. They can do a wide range of jobs and can be deployed alongside their full-time counterparts overseas in peacekeeping and other duties.

▶ Jobs in the emergency services

Emergency service jobs include the blue light services such as the Police Service, Ambulance Service, and Fire and Rescue Service. Like their military counterparts, there is a range of different sorts of roles you can do in this branch of the services, including operational, non-operational, civilian support and voluntary roles.

Operational roles

Operational roles are those which deliver front line emergency services to the public. They include roles such as police officer, paramedic, firefighter and coastguard.

Role case study

Her Majesty's (HM) Coastguard – coastguard rescue officer

People working as operational coastguards coordinate maritime search and rescue within the UK coastal area, which includes over 10,500 nautical miles of coastline. This includes people in distress at sea or on oil rigs, or emergencies on the coast or shoreline. They also keep people and vessels safe by marking dangerous areas, inspecting ships and boats to ensure they meet safety standards, and providing safety certificates for boats, ships and the people working on them.

Entrance requirements

- 16 years of age or over
- A good standard of literacy and numeracy, and IT and typing skills
- Good hearing and eyesight
- Extensive seagoing experience

Activity 3.3   Job opportunities in the Police Service

It can be very difficult to get a job in the Police Service. What are the advantages and disadvantages of working in the Police Service? Why do you think so many people want to be police officers? What are the main types of work they do?

Produce a short booklet outlining the job opportunities in the Police Service and covering their advantages and disadvantages. Finish by evaluating whether you are suited to the Police Service and what skills you might need.

Just checking

1 What are the differences between operational roles and non-operational roles?

2 What types of jobs can civilians do in the armed services?

3 What does HM Coastguard do?

Non-operational roles

Non-operational roles in the emergency services are those which have less direct contact with emergency situations. They can cover a variety of jobs such as:

- educating the community on safety, crime prevention or health matters
- non-paramedic ambulance staff.

Role case study

Police Service – family liaison officer

Where a serious crime, such as murder or abduction, has occurred, this specialist role in the Police Service acts as the primary link between the police and the victim's family. Family liaison officers are trained to gather material from the family to help the investigation and keep the family up to date with developments, while also supporting them as much as possible and gaining their confidence and trust. They can also help to deal with the media if the family need support.

Entrance requirements

- Must be a serving police officer
- Must have the approval of your line manager
- Must have completed specific training courses

Civilian support roles

There are lots of civilian support roles in the emergency services including:

- control room operators
- incident managers
- scenes of crime officers
- community support officers.

Role case study

Ambulance Service – ambulance care assistant

Ambulance care assistants transport disabled, elderly, sick or vulnerable people to and from routine hospital appointments, outpatient clinics or day care centres. Ambulance care assistants are based at an ambulance station or hospital with a team of other assistants. You might work on your own or with another care assistant, depending on the type of vehicle you drive. You will cover a particular local area and might have to work shifts.

Entrance requirements

- A good general education (can vary between ambulance trusts)
- Full manual driving licence with appropriate licence classifications

Police Service – police community support officer (PCSO)

A PCSO is a civilian who acts as a visible presence on the streets of local areas where anti-social behaviour is a problem. They perform some of the same duties as a patrol constable, dealing with anti-social behaviour such as graffiti, truancy, litter and nuisance. Their presence can help reduce fear of crime among the public. They also:

- support victims of crime
- protect the public
- assist with house-to-house enquiries
- detain suspects until a police constable arrives
- direct traffic and remove abandoned vehicles.

PCSOs complement the work of the traditional police constable by focusing on lower level crime, so that the police can focus on more serious crime.

Entrance requirements

- No formal education requirements, but must be able to pass written tests
- Physically and mentally able to undertake the role, including good eyesight
- Some tattoos and facial piercings may disqualify you
- Some criminal convictions and cautions may disqualify you

Activity 3.4   Scenes of crime officers

Scenes of crime officers (SOCOs) find, collect and record forensic evidence. Their role also includes crime scene photography and video. Many people think that scenes of crime officers are police officers with special training, but the majority are actually civilians who work alongside the Police Service.

1 Research the role of a civilian scenes of crime officer. What qualifications do you need to be accepted for training?

2 What kind of work would you do?

3 Where would you find job opportunities like this advertised?

Discussion

Why do you think the emergency services use volunteers to help them achieve their objectives? What do you think are the advantages and disadvantages of using volunteers?

Voluntary support roles

There are several different types of voluntary support roles in the emergency services such as:

- Mountain Rescue volunteer
- police special constable
- St John Ambulance volunteer.

Role case study

Police Service – special constable

There are around 19,000 special constables working alongside full-time officers in England and Wales. They may do other jobs, and only have to work a certain number of hours a week as a special constable. Special constables undertake a wide range of work, including conducting foot patrols, providing security at major events, educating young people about crime reduction and community protection, and assisting at incident scenes.

Entrance requirements

- Aged 18 or over
- Reasonably fit and healthy
- Able to pass written tests
- Mentally and physically fit enough to undertake the requirements of the role
- Most convictions or cautions would make you ineligible

▶ Jobs in the local authority

Local authorities are often one of the largest employers in any particular geographical area. The roles available include:

- education welfare officer
- leisure assistant
- refuse collector
- housing officer.

Role case study

Local authority – housing officer

Housing officers supervise the day-to-day management and maintenance of rented properties that belong to the local authority. These properties are often referred to as social housing or council housing. Responsibilities can include allocating accommodation, inspecting properties, dealing with problem tenants, ensuring rents are paid and attending tenants' meetings.

Entrance requirements

- No formal entrance requirements, but many housing officers are qualified to A level standard or equivalent

Role case study

Local authority – refuse collector

As a refuse collector, you are responsible for removing waste and recyclable material from homes and businesses and taking it away to be disposed of or recycled. You normally work as part of a small team and in all weathers.

Entrance requirements

- No formal entrance requirements, but you need to be fit as the work is physical
- To drive the collection lorry you need to have a Large Goods Vehicle licence

Take it further

Research the role of a probation officer and the support staff they employ. What do they do and what are the entrance requirements?

National Probation Service (NPS)

Although the probation service does not report to the local authority, it does work closely with them. It is the service that manages offenders after they have been released from prison or as part of their sentence.

▶ Central government

There are many jobs available in central government such as management and technical roles, or specific roles in particular government departments such as the Ministry of Defence or the Ministry of Justice. Jobs include roles such as clerk to the court, who advises magistrates on the law when they are sentencing people in court, and administrative officers who keep court records.

Activity 3.5　Central government jobs

Central government jobs range from the civil service to the courts service and government ministries such as the Ministry of Defence. In pairs, consider the jobs available in central government and their entrance requirements. Are they attractive to you? Explain your answer.

▶ Know the conditions of service in different public services

Introduction

Conditions of service are very important to consider when looking for jobs in the public services. They determine the amount you will be paid, the holidays you can take and when you can retire. Have you considered the conditions of service in the organisation you want to join?

Conditions of service are the rules you agree to abide by when you join an organisation. They are the agreed terms of your employment and include your:

- salary – the amount you will be paid (the services normally pay you on a monthly basis)
- salary structure – the different levels of salary paid to people in a service, where the amount that you are paid increases with your experience or the length of time you have been in the job
- holiday entitlement – the amount of annual leave you can have
- benefits – some employers provide free access to gyms, accommodation and private medical insurance
- retirement age – some services have variable retirement ages

- pension arrangements – pensions are really important, because the money you pay into your pension while working will be the money you have to live on when you retire
- sick pay – the amount of money you will be paid if you need to be off work because you are sick
- maternity/paternity provision – the amount of time you can have off and the pay you will receive upon the birth or adoption of a child
- shift patterns – how your working hours will be spread across the week or month (remember, the services often have to provide 24-hour cover)
- access to training and/or education – personal and professional development is very important in the public services as it allows you to do your job well.

The conditions of service differ from service to service and also differ between the individual jobs within a service. This can make it difficult to compare conditions of service.

Activity 3.6   Terms and conditions

Public services have different terms and conditions that they offer to new candidates. Research the service you are hoping to join and identify:

- starting salary
- usual working hours
- pension arrangements
- annual leave
- shift patterns.

Does any of this information influence your decision to join the service? Do you think the service you have chosen provides good terms and conditions? Write up your thoughts.

Assessment activity 3.1   *English*

You need to organise a careers day for your school or college so that people who are interested in a career in the public services can speak to members of the services to find out more about opportunities available and entrance requirements.

Produce a series of posters which include information about three different public services and the work they undertake. For each public service, include:

- the advantages and disadvantages of working in that service
- three different specific job roles within that service
- the entrance requirements and conditions of service.

As part of your careers day, you should be ready to answer questions and provide people with additional information if they need it.

Tips

- Make sure your careers day is interesting and engaging by thinking about what people want to know.
- Remember to cover services from different groups.

POLICE

▶ Application and selection processes of the public services for employment

Introduction

If you are planning to apply to a public service you will need to know how to apply. Each service will have a different application and selection procedure. Procedures can also change every few years, so it is worth speaking to a recruiting officer to make sure the information you have for your service is accurate and up to date.

The purpose of the application and selection process is to ensure that:

- each service is able to recruit the right type of person for each job
- each service is able to test the skills of the candidates to ensure they can operate successfully in that service.

▶ Application process requirements

To get a job in a public service, you must meet their application process requirements. These may include:

- meeting the entry requirements
- completing the application form
- providing supporting written evidence, such as references
- providing a CV.

Entry requirements

Entry requirements specify the minimum personal and professional achievements that you should have before applying to a public service. These can be factors such as education, fitness and health. The more specialised the role, the more entry requirements will be asked for.

In some cases, it may be a case of waiting until you are old enough to join, but while you are waiting you could do things which make you more attractive to a public service, such as getting additional qualifications at college or doing voluntary work in the community.

Whenever you consider applying to a public service, remember that there are many other people who also want that particular job. These people may have more experience and qualifications than you and you must compete with them for the role. As you can imagine, this can be difficult, but the key is good preparation. For an example of a recruitment process, see the case study on page 89.

Application forms

An application form is a set of written questions asked by an employer so that they can assess your suitability for a job and decide whether they should invite you for interview. Application forms can be paper-based or online. For more information on application forms, see page 95.

Additional written documentation

Sometimes public sector employers will want you to provide some additional information about yourself. This may mean providing some or all of the following documents.

- Letter of application – this is a letter to an employer which is sometimes used instead of a CV. It lists all your previous experience and qualifications and also tells the employer why you want the job and what skills you have to offer.
- Personal statement – this is your opportunity to tell the service you are applying to why you want to work with them and why they should hire you. It can be the most difficult part of an application to write.
- Supporting information – this is any information which supports your application, including references.

? Did you know?

Examples of good practice in giving answers can sometimes be found on public services' own websites.

Activity 3.7 — Personal statements

Personal statements can be the most difficult part of application forms to write. Choose a public services job vacancy and write a 200-word personal statement which summarises the achievements in your life so far.

A CV

CV stands for 'curriculum vitae' and it is typically a one or two page overview of a person's experience and qualifications. For more information on CVs, see pages 96–97.

Case study

The Police Service is difficult to get into because of the high number of applicants. The selection process is thorough and tests a number of different skills to make sure you are fit to be a police officer. This process includes several stages.

1 Your details are checked to make sure you meet the entrance requirements.

2 If you meet the requirements, your application form will be marked.

3 If your application form is good enough, you will attend an assessment centre.

4 If you are successful at the assessment centre, you will undergo a number of checks, including medical and eyesight checks.

5 Background checks will be made and references will be taken.

6 You will attend a medical examination and complete a physical fitness test.

7 Your joining date will be agreed.

The assessment centre contains a variety of exercises, including:

- a competency-based interview
- a numeracy test
- a verbal ability test
- two written exercises
- four interactive exercises.

1 What do you think the police recruitment process is designed to achieve?

2 Do you think the activities are well-matched to the skills needed as a police officer?

3 What would you need to do to prepare yourself for this process?

▶ Selection processes

Selection processes often involve more than just application forms and CVs. You may also have to take several tests and attend interviews.

Testing

Some tests used by the public services are shown in Table 3.2.

However, tests do not provide an employer with a face-to-face picture of a candidate. This means that tests are likely to occur before a formal interview and are used as a method of weeding out unsuitable or poorly qualified candidates.

Table 3.2: Tests used in selection processes.

Type of test	Description
Psychometric tests	Tell your potential employer about your character. They can be broken into two types: • **ability and aptitude** tests (focus on what a person can currently do and the potential they have) • **personality tests** (assess what a person is actually like).
Basic skills tests	Test your: • literacy • numeracy • IT skills.
Competency tests	Test a particular skill or behaviour, such as decision-making, dealing with pressure and leadership.
Role play and simulations	Used by employers to assess your interpersonal skills and problem solving ability, especially in difficult situations.
Presentations	Show your ability to speak in public and communicate information effectively to others. You may need to give a presentation on a particular public service topic (up to 10 minutes long).
Physical fitness tests	Assess your fitness and suitability for certain jobs, especially in the emergency and armed services.

Link

Public service fitness tests are covered in more detail in Unit 5, pages 156–158.

Case study

The Royal Navy has a thorough application and selection process, which has several stages.

- Complete a short eligibility questionnaire to be sure you are eligible to join.
- Attend a careers presentation to learn more about the Royal Navy.
- Complete a short application form.
- Sit the Royal Navy recruitment test, covering basic English, maths, problem solving and mechanical skills.
- Attend a formal interview.
- Attend a medical and an eye examination.
- Complete the Royal Navy pre-joining fitness test.
- Attend the Royal Navy pre-joining course.
- Take up a place as a rating at HMS Raleigh.

1 Why would the Royal Navy require you to have good English, maths and problem solving skills?

2 What is the importance of the medical and eye examination?

3 How does this process compare with the Police Service application and selection process on page 88?

Did you know?

The Royal Navy pre-joining course includes a swimming test. You need to be able to jump into deep water wearing overalls, tread water for two minutes, then swim 50m and climb out at the end.

Equal opportunity – ensuring diversity

Diversity means variety and describes the range of visible and non-visible differences that exist between people. These differences include gender, skin colour, hair type, sexuality, religion and disability. We are all different from each other and we should value these differences rather than discriminate against them.

The services value diversity because a diverse workforce has a variety of skills and strengths which can help when dealing with specific communities in the UK or in conflict situations. These skills and strengths include:

- additional languages
- cultural knowledge
- religious awareness.

For the services, diversity is about valuing our differences as a way to make the service more efficient and effective.

Activity 3.8   Diversity in the Police Service

According to police workforce statistics for 2013, the Police Service in England and Wales includes:

- 6,555 ethnic minority officers, which is 5% of all police officers
- 35,471 female officers, which is 27% of all police officers.

What could the Police Service do to make itself a more attractive career option to women and people from ethnic minorities? Create an advertising campaign to encourage more women and people from ethnic minorities to apply to the Police Service.

Although attitudes towards diversity in the public services are changing, more needs to be done. This includes encouraging women, people from ethnic minorities and other under-represented groups to apply, as well as ensuring that they have opportunities to progress in their career and will not be discriminated against.

Why do you think it is important that the public services respect equality and diversity?

Interviews

There are many different types of interview that you might face when applying to a public service. These include formal interviews, group interviews and panel interviews, as shown in Table 3.3.

Table 3.3: Different types of interview.

Interview type	Details
Formal	• Structured interview. • Likely to be a set series of questions in a formal setting. • Likely to be conducted by more than one interviewer. • May have to produce a presentation or report to bring to the interview.
Informal	• More relaxed interview, in a less formal setting than a formal interview. • May be conducted by one or two interviewers rather than a panel.
Full day	• Can last up to 10 hours, including interviews and activities. • Likely to interact with other applicants competing for the same job.
Multi-day	• Common in the public services. • May have to be interviewed on three or more days over a period of several weeks.
Panel	• Conducted by a panel of up to six or seven interviewers. • Each interviewer may assess you on different aspects of your performance and then discuss their findings after the interview.
Individual	• Conducted by a single interviewer. • Not considered good practice because there is no second opinion.

Dress code

You must dress appropriately for interviews. This usually means a suit for both men and women. Jewellery and make-up must be subtle and discreet. You should not wear any facial piercings (such as eyebrow, nose or lip) and men should consider removing earrings. Your clothing should be clean and pressed.

Remember

Get a friend or family member to check you over before you set off for your interview.

Preparing for your interview

It is your responsibility to find out what you are likely to face and to prepare for it. The other applicants will be prepared, so do not let yourself down.

One key aspect of interview preparation is **knowing the interview arrangements**. Ask yourself the following questions.

- Where is the interview?
- What time should you be there?
- What do you need to take with you?
- Have you confirmed your attendance?
- Do you know what to wear?
- Have you researched the organisation so you know what they do and how they do it?
- Have you brushed up on your interview skills?
- What are they likely to ask you?

Most **interview questions** are fairly standard. You can expect to be asked some or all of the following questions.

- Why do you want this job?
- What can you bring to the job?
- Describe how your previous experience makes you suitable for this job.
- What do you hope to gain from the job?
- What do you know about the job?
- Do you know about current developments affecting the job?
- Are you able to work as an individual and as a team member?
- What are your long-term career goals?
- What training and education do you have which would enable you to do this job effectively?
- What are your views on equal opportunities?

Before you go to your interview, prepare your own answers to these questions and any other questions that you can think of. You may be asked about something you wrote in your CV or covering letter, so read them again before you go.

When you go for an interview, **your interview skills** are a key part of your performance. Interviewers will assess you on your knowledge and the answers you give, but they will also be looking out for the following elements, because they indicate how professional you are likely to be:

- punctuality – allow enough time so you can get there early, so you have time to prepare yourself when you arrive
- your appearance – make sure you dress smartly, polish your shoes, tuck your shirt in, brush your hair, etc.
- your body language – this speaks volumes about your attitude, so sit up straight, and look alert
- listening and speaking skills – make sure you listen carefully to the questions you are being asked, and be clear when giving your answers. Do not use slang.

Activity 3.9

Interview questions

You will be asked lots of questions during the selection process, such as:

'Please give a specific example of a task, project or responsibility you have undertaken that you are particularly proud of.'

How would you answer this question?

Working in pairs, ask each other this question and assess each other's answer.

Job-searching techniques

Introduction

Finding a job to apply for can sometimes be as difficult as the application and selection procedure itself, especially if you do not know where to look. There are several things you can do to maximise your chances of finding a suitable vacancy.

Different career paths

There are many different career paths in the public services. These include the emergency services, the armed services, local and central government and the voluntary services. It helps to know which service and what types of job you are interested in before you start to search.

Using criteria for job searches

Some jobs may have requirements which you are not prepared to meet, for example if you are a carer or a young parent you may not be able to be posted away from home. This may mean that the armed services are not for you. You may want to earn over £20,000 per year as a starting salary, which might mean you choose not to join the armed services, where starting salaries are generally about £14,000. These criteria will be personal to you, but it is important to consider them when looking for jobs.

Auditing and matching your skills

Before you start to look for public service jobs, you should assess your own strengths and weaknesses. You can do this by conducting a skills audit or SWOT analysis. This will help you to see which jobs or services you are most suited to and what you can do to improve your chances of getting a job in your chosen service. This is especially useful in the public services because it is a competitive sector.

Link

For more information and an example of a SWOT analysis, see Unit 2 page 62.

Recognising suitable opportunities

It is important to apply only for suitable opportunities, rather than for every vacancy in your chosen service. You may see an advertisement for a job and think you can apply for it, but it is important to know whether you will need a certain set of skills or whether you can pick up these skills on the job. For example, you cannot apply for a job as a nurse unless you are actually qualified, because it is not a role you can learn on the job. However, you could apply for a role such as an ambulance care assistant and learn on the job.

▶ Places to search for vacancies

The best place to search for any job vacancy is the internet. Most organisations advertise vacancies on their own websites, as well as on specialist recruitment websites.

Local and national newspapers can be good sources of job vacancies. They will often list local authority, charity and central government vacancies. Trade journals are the specific magazines for particular industries, which most professionals in the industry will read, though not all services advertise in trade journals. You may also see national advertising campaigns, particularly for the armed services, who regularly recruit new people.

Activity 3.10	Job vacancies

Job vacancies are advertised on each service's website. Find out about the official website for the service of your choice, and locate the vacancies page.

▶ CVs and application forms

Introduction

You will have to complete an application form and prepare a CV for many public service jobs. Do you have any experience of applying for jobs, or know about the skills that this requires? In this topic you will build your skills so that you will know what to do and be more confident when you apply for a job.

▶ Making a good application

Like any other skill, you need to practise completing application forms and producing CVs. There are some things you should always think about when you are doing this, as shown in Table 3.4.

Table 3.4: Things to remember when completing application forms or writing your CV.

Structure and layout	• Must be neat and professional. • Always use formal tone and language.
Personal knowledge, skills and experience	• Show how your knowledge, skills and experience match the job you are applying for. • Show that you will be able to do the job.
Specific knowledge, technical ability, education or training	• Show your level of education and any relevant technical abilities. • Technical abilities could include first aid, ability to drive, ability to operate specific equipment or specific skills needed in the job. • Summarise your skills clearly so that an employer will immediately understand them.

continued

Table 3.4 continued

Relevant work experience and hobbies or interests	• Do not list all your work experience or interests – only list things which are relevant to the job you are applying for.
Interest and motivation	• Explain why you want the job and what motivates you to join this particular service.

Application forms

An application form is a document where you record all the personal information the service needs to know about you. They then use this information to make judgements about whether you are suitable for the service. Application forms are normally available from the recruiting office of your chosen service or from their website.

Depending on the service, the application form may ask for some or all of the following information:

- name
- address
- contact details
- nationality
- convictions and cautions
- tattoos
- health and eyesight
- business interests
- financial position
- previous addresses
- details about your immediate family (if relevant to the job)
- previous employment details and references
- education, qualifications and training
- a competence assessment which asks you about situations you have been involved in and how you reacted, including equality and diversity situations
- why you want to join the service
- what you expect the job to be like
- how you have prepared for your job application
- an equal opportunities questionnaire
- a personal statement
- a health assessment (if relevant to the job).

Completing an application form takes time and effort. If you complete the form incorrectly or it shows you in a poor light you will be weeded out in what is called a **paper sift**.

Completing an application form

There are several things that you can do to make sure you have the best chance of success:

- read the form thoroughly and make sure you understand every question
- read the guidance notes – they will give you advice on what you need to do
- photocopy the form several times so that you can practise and get it checked by a tutor or someone similar before you fill out the original
- be honest – if you lie, it will be found out and you could even ruin your chances of getting a job in the service you want to join

 Key term

Paper sift – a way of removing unsuitable applications, used by many public services and other employers. It involves checking application forms and weeding out any forms that are incomplete, show a poor standard of English, or demonstrate that the individual is unsuitable for the job.

- pay attention to your spelling and grammar
- ensure the things you write do not breach the principles of equality and diversity
- take guidance from your local careers office or your tutors on how best to present yourself
- use the appropriate style of writing. If the form says to use black ink and block capitals, then this is what you must do. Make sure that your handwriting is clear and legible.

Activity 3.11   Application form

Most public services have their application forms on their websites. Find the application form for the service you are most interested in and have a go at completing it. What was difficult? What did you find easy? What will you do to improve before you complete it for real?

▶ Curriculum vitae (CV)

You will probably be asked to produce a CV at some point in your application procedure for any service, and it is important that your CV is up to date and relevant to your application. A CV is not just a list of your personal information but a demonstration of your suitability for the job. Figure 3.3 and Figure 3.4 are two CVs with identical information. However, the first is an example of how not to do it, while the second is an example of good practice.

Name:	Jamille Hussain
Address:	27 Springfield Drive, Lakeshire, LA5 6XX
Telephone Number:	01632 960312
E-mail:	jamrox@spotmail.co.uk
Date of Birth:	1/1/1997
Marital status:	Single, but have a girlfreind
Driving Lisense:	I do not drive, but I am taking lessons
School:	Lakeshire Compreensive I passed 3 GCSE's
	• Maths D • Endlish D • French F
	I have also completed a Btec Fitst Diploma in Public services at Lakeshire College
Work experiences:	I have woked in a local supermarket and done a paper round. I also do some roofing with my dad and help at a local youth club
References:	
Zalini Wrynne	Foodbusters
Lakeshire Youth Club	101 high Street
Lakeshire	Lakeshire

Figure 3.3: What would you do to improve this CV?

Activity 3.12   Jamille's CV

Look carefully at Figure 3.3. How many things can you find that are wrong with it? Make a list and compare your list with your classmates' lists.

Curriculum Vitae

Jamille Hussain

A hard working and energetic young man, well able to cope with working in a high pressure environment under specific time constraints. Excellent interpersonal skills and a high level of experience in working with the public in a variety of situations. Excels in a variety of sports and has a high level of commitment to working with the community.

Personal Details:

Address: 27 Springfield Drive, Lakeshire, LA5 6XX
Telephone: 01632 960312 (Home)   07700 900671 (Mobile)
Email: jhussain17@spotmail.co.uk
Date of Birth: 1/1/97

Educational Achievements:

2012 – 2013   Lakeshire College of Further Education, Lower Redridge, Lakeshire LA5 4TY

BTEC First Award in Public Services
* The Role and Work of the Public Services   Distinction
* Working Skills in the Public Service Sector   Distinction
* Employment in the Public Services   Merit
* Health, Fitness and Lifestyle for the Public Services   Distinction

2007 – 2012   Lakeshire Comprehensive School, Main Street, Lakeshire, LA3 4EW

* Physical Education A
* Geography C
* Maths D
* English D
* French F

I also achieved 100% attendance certificates for every year I attended Lakeshire Comprehensive and I won the Connor Rivers Award for excellence in sporting achievement in 2010 and 2011.

Career Achievements:

Jan 2013 – Present   *Volunteer Youth Worker*

I volunteer three evenings a week to help at a youth club in my local area. This involved coordinating and running sporting events for young people aged 11–14, improving their sporting skills and ensuring that health and safety guidelines are followed. I enjoy this type of work very much and like to think that I act as a positive role model for the young people I train.

Dec 2012 – Present   *Builder's Labourer*

In this position I work as part of an interconnected team of roofers and builders adhering to strict deadlines and producing high quality work. My teamwork skills were enhanced and I developed an appreciation of how people working together can achieve more than individuals working alone.

July 2012 – Dec 2012   *Shop Worker*

Working on a checkout with speed and efficiency. I interacted with the public on an ongoing basis providing a friendly and reliable front of house service as well as observing health and hygiene regulations.

Sept 2011 – June 2012   *Newspaper Delivery Operative*

This position involved the delivery of early morning and evening newspapers on a set route. I developed my time management skills and self discipline fulfilling this role as I had to be very conscious of making sure I delivered all of the goods regardless of external conditions such as the weather.

Additional Information

I have played football and cricket for the county under-18s teams and I enjoy a variety of other sporting and adventurous activities such as skiing, climbing and canoeing. I like to go to the cinema, particularly to see science fiction films and to socialise with my friends. I have recently started to attend ju-jitsu classes and I hope this will enhance my physical coordination and sense of self discipline. I am looking for a career opportunity where I can work with people in a community environment as I feel that this is what my skills and inclination best suit me for.

References

Ms Alison Court   Mr A J Singh
Lecturer in Public Services   Youth Services Manager
Lakeshire College of FE   Lakeshire Youth Club
Lower Redridge   Murray Road
Lakeshire   Lakeshire
LA5 4TY   LA7 9LU

Figure 3.4: Would you organise your CV in this way?

Activity 3.13   Comparing the CVs

1 What are the differences between the two examples of CV? Which one do you think employers are likely to prefer and why?

2 Using Figure 3.4 as a template, create your own CV which showcases your achievements.

Assessment activity 3.2

Finding a suitable job in the public services can be a challenge. There are lots of public services to choose from and each service has lots of jobs within it. You need to develop the skills to find vacancies and assess whether they are suitable for you.

You will research the application and selection procedures used for two jobs in the public sector, and write a report on your findings. Make sure you choose jobs from contrasting public services, and discuss the differences and similarities in the application and selection processes.

Use your job-searching techniques to investigate two job opportunities from different public services. Then evaluate your suitability for the roles and decide which one best suits you and your skills. Consider how you might improve your skills. Say why the job you have chosen is the most suitable. Include all of these details in your report.

Produce a written application for the job you have chosen. It should show how you meet all the requirements of the job.

Tips

- Make sure your application looks professional, using correct English and the right tone.
- Remember that your application is your opportunity to show your skills and abilities.
- It is also important to evaluate your own suitability for the jobs you have researched. 'Evaluate' means to bring together the information you have found and use it to come to a conclusion. Always give evidence to support your conclusion.
- Be prepared to say how you suit one job more than another and what you might be able to do to improve your skills.

WorkSpace

▶ Alex Seagrave

Retained firefighter

I'm a retained firefighter at a rural fire station in Yorkshire. Along with my colleagues, I'm responsible for responding to emergency call-outs and doing the usual things you would associate with a regular firefighter, such as:

- putting out fires
- responding to road traffic incidents
- saving lives and property.

Retained firefighters are part-time firefighters who respond to emergency call-outs. When I get a call I have five minutes to respond and get to the station. I enjoy working as a retained firefighter. I own a local business and I'm local to the area, so it's nice to be able to give something back to a community I know so well.

It is too expensive to have a fully operational fire station where we are as it would only serve a couple of small local communities, but the area still needs fire service cover. That's where retained firefighters come in. We are a vital public service for small communities and I'm very proud of what we do.

I wouldn't really want to be a full-time firefighter as I enjoy owning and running my own business, but working this way allows me to have the best of both worlds.

Think about it

1 What are the advantages of having retained firefighters?

2 Why does Alex think being a retained firefighter is the best of both worlds?

3 What do you think would be the challenges in juggling a full-time job and being a retained firefighter?

Introduction

There are lots of public services that work to protect our communities. You would probably identify the emergency services and armed services as the most important, but there are many other services within local authorities and the voluntary sector which play an important role in community protection.

The UK is a multi-cultural society made up of a range of different communities, including religious, cultural, geographical and ethnic communities. This unit examines how the public services work to protect the interests of different communities as well as the nation as a whole.

The public services also need to work together as a team to manage the hazards and risks found in local communities. Risks that the public services have to deal with include flooding, waste disposal and protecting vulnerable individuals.

Over five million people work in the UK public sector, providing services to ensure that we are safe and supported. This unit will explore the key things that they do to ensure our safety and security.

Assessment: This unit will be assessed through a series of assignments set by your tutor/teacher.

Learning aims

In this unit you will:

A explore the key organisations involved in the protection of communities

B understand how hazards and risks to individuals and communities are managed by the public services.

> I didn't realise how much work the public services do to keep our communities safe. I knew about the emergency services and their roles, but I was really surprised by the role of charities and volunteers and how they support and protect us. There are also a lot of risks and hazards faced by local communities that I hadn't considered. I'm much more aware of all these issues in my local area now.
>
> Hassan, *15-year-old police cadet*

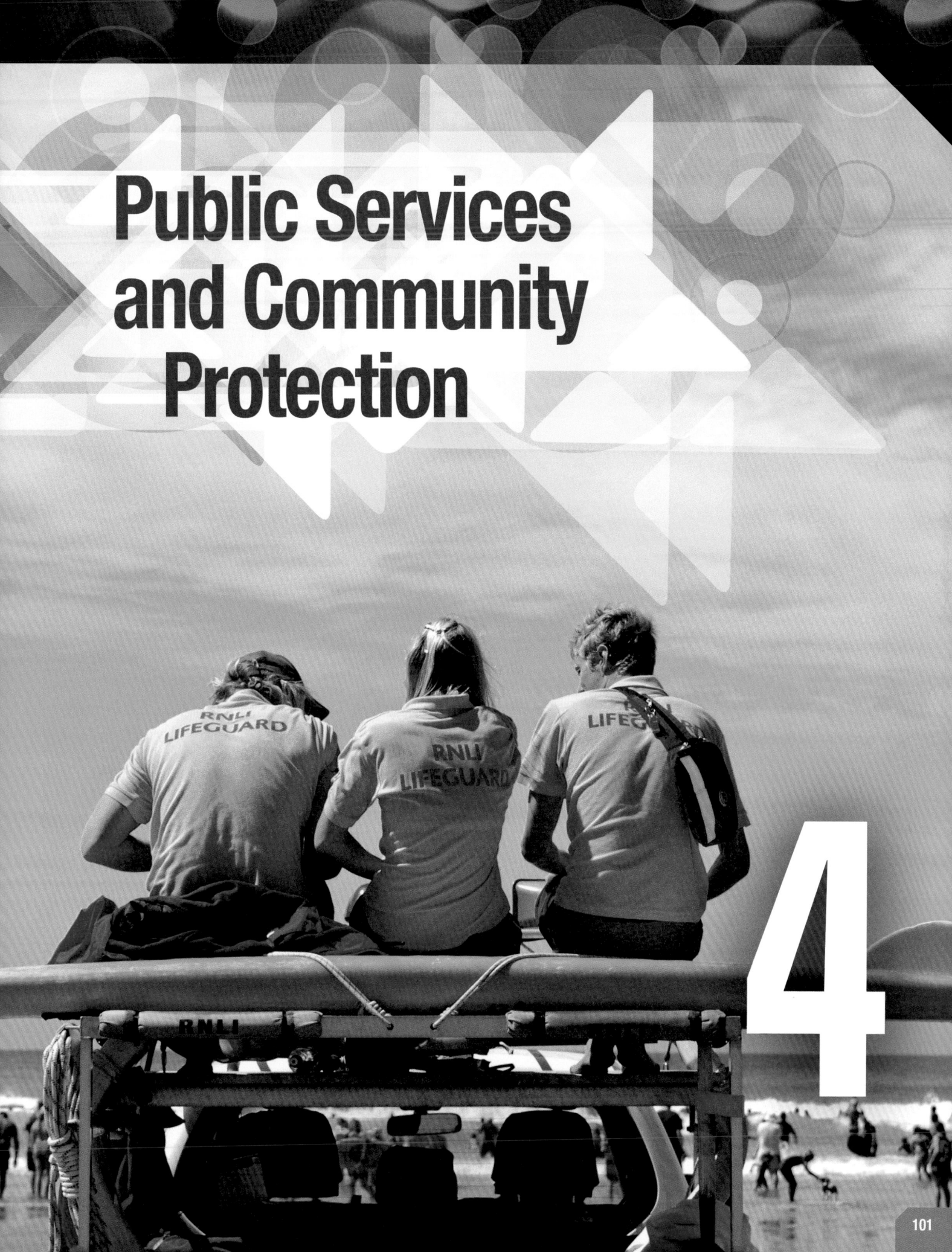

Public Services and Community Protection

BTEC
Assessment Zone

This table shows you what you must do in order to achieve a **Pass**, **Merit** or **Distinction** grade, and where you can find activities to help you.

Assessment criteria

Level 1	Level 2 Pass	Level 2 Merit	Level 2 Distinction
Learning aim A: Explore the key organisations involved in the protection of communities			
1A.1 Identify the needs of two different types of communities.	**2A.P1** Describe the needs of two different types of communities. **See Assessment activity 4.1, page 115**	**2A.M1** Compare, using examples, the ways in which two contrasting public services work to protect their community. **See Assessment activity 4.1, page 115**	**2A.D1** Analyse the advantages to the local community of two contrasting public services working together to protect their community. **See Assessment activity 4.1, page 115**
1A.2 Outline the ways in which two contrasting public services work to protect communities.	**2A.P2** Explain how two contrasting public services work to protect different types of communities. **See Assessment activity 4.1, page 115**		
Learning aim B: Understand how hazards and risks to individuals and communities are managed by the public services			
1B.3 Outline the different types of potential hazards and risks in communities.	**2B.P3** Describe how communities manage hazards and risks. **See Assessment activity 4.2, page 128**	**2B.M2** Explain the potential benefits of contingency planning for managing hazards and risks in communities, using examples. **See Assessment activity 4.2, page 128**	
1B.4 Identify ways in which individuals can support the public services in managing risks within the community.	**2B.P4** Describe ways in which individuals support the public services in managing risks within the community. **See Assessment activity 4.2, page 128**	**2B.M3** Explain the benefits of individuals supporting the public services in managing risks within the community. **See Assessment activity 4.2, page 128**	**2B.D2** Analyse, using specific examples, the benefits of individuals supporting the public services in managing risks within the community. **See Assessment activity 4.2, page 128**
1B.5 Identify how the public services work together to protect the community from one hazard or risk.	**2B.P5** Explain how one type of multi-agency working protects the community from risks and hazards. **See Assessment activity 4.2, page 128**	**2B.M4** Assess one way in which the public services work together to protect the community from risks and hazards. **See Assessment activity 4.2, page 128**	**2B.D3** Evaluate ways in which the public services work together to protect the community from risks and hazards. **See Assessment activity 4.2, page 128**

How you will be assessed

This unit will be assessed by a series of assignments set by your tutor. You will need to explore the key organisations which have a role in protecting communities and understand the range of risks and hazards that are faced by communities and managed by the public services.

Your assessment could be in the form of:

- a magazine article
- an information booklet
- a poster
- a presentation
- a report.

▶ Types of communities

Introduction

The public services serve a wide range of individuals and communities. Have you ever considered the different types of communities that exist in the UK and the services they need from the public sector? What communities can you think of? What services do they need most?

Communities can be defined in many ways. Some people believe that communities are groups of people who share the same local area, while others believe that communities have shared beliefs and cultures. In general, communities can be grouped into six types, as shown in Figure 4.1.

Discussion

Consider the communities shown in Figure 4.1. Which of these do you think you belong to? Discuss why the communities you belong to are important to you. Make a note of your main points.

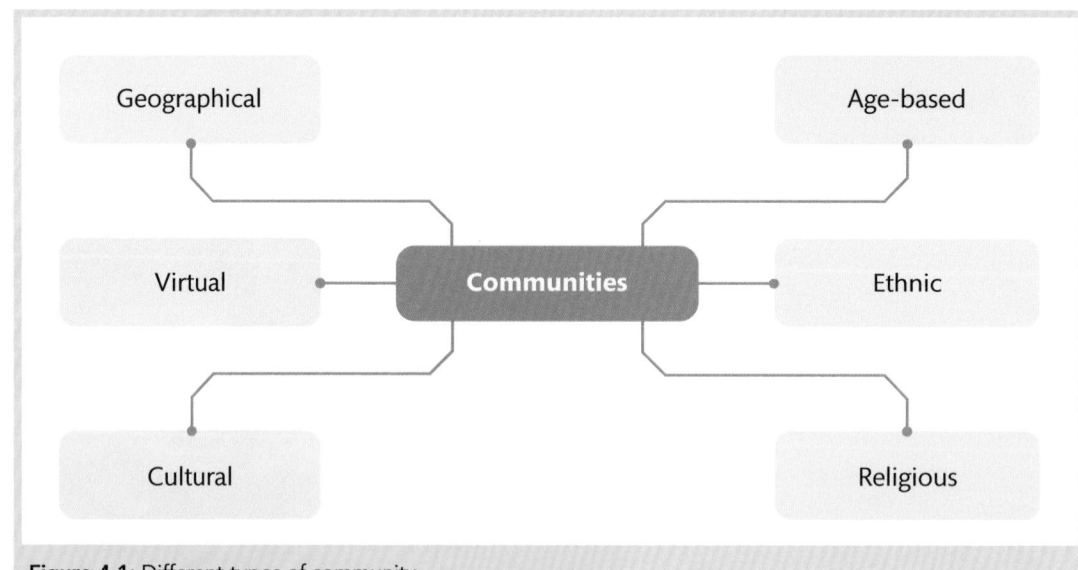

Figure 4.1: Different types of community.

▶ Geographical communities

A geographical community is a group of people living in the same geographical area for a considerable period of time. It could be an area as small as a street or group of streets, or it could be as large as a town or city. Military bases, submarines or ships could also be thought of as communities, since the people in them are likely to spend a lot of time together relatively isolated from others.

Sometimes, the geography of an area leads to it being isolated from other areas, e.g. on an island or in a valley. This can help to create a sense of community.

Local authorities serve geographical communities such as towns, parishes, districts, cities or counties. They provide services specifically for the people of that area. The emergency services also operate on a regional basis, but the regions are often bigger than those of local councils. For example, Sheffield City Council provides the local services needed to support the city of Sheffield, but South Yorkshire Police provide policing services to the whole county, which includes other towns such as Barnsley, Rotherham and Doncaster. However, Yorkshire Ambulance Service provides services to *all* Yorkshire counties, including North Yorkshire, South Yorkshire and West Yorkshire.

Geographical communities need protection from a number of different issues, including illness and anti-social behaviour.

Protection from illness

Like most communities, geographical communities need protection from illness. This is why most geographical communities have a range of health services within easy travelling distance. These health services include:

- dental surgeries
- GP surgeries
- pharmacies
- health visitors
- opticians
- **antenatal** care and midwives.

In addition, the NHS, local authority and other public services offer a range of health-related services to which you may have to travel further, such as:

- mental health services
- hospitals
- environmental health services.

Discussion

Public services deal with different sizes of community. For example, Yorkshire Ambulance Service provides emergency response to an area with over 5 million people in it. Do you think this can be called a community? At what point does an area become too big to be a geographical community?

Key term

Antenatal – before birth, or relating to pregnancy.

Case study

The environmental health department of your local council aims to protect the local community, across a range of health, hygiene and safety issues including:

- food safety and hygiene
- industrial pollution
- commercial waste
- contaminated land
- pest control
- noise and odour
- animal welfare (dog wardens)
- workplace health and safety
- cemeteries.

The department aims to safeguard residents, traders and visitors to the area by protecting their health, safety and environment. This includes the air they breathe, the food they buy and their safety in the workplace. They also ensure that pests, refuse and noise are controlled.

1 Why do you think we need a local service such as environmental health?

2 What would happen if we did not have services like this?

3 Describe some of the ways in which environmental health departments protect communities from illness.

Discussion

Do you know of an area that experiences anti-social behaviour? Could the way you behave when you are out with your friends upset or frighten people? Discuss these questions, considering the impact that anti-social behaviour can have on a community.

Did you know?

Anti-social behaviour is estimated to cost the UK around £3.4 billion per year, according to the National Audit Office.

Protection from crime and anti-social behaviour

Crime and anti-social behaviour can cause great misery in local communities. Crime can include domestic violence, burglary and car crime. Anti-social behaviour is lower level crime that can ruin the quality of life for others, such as:

- graffiti and vandalism
- littering or dumping rubbish
- misusing fireworks, including using them late at night
- shouting or noisy behaviour in places where this might be annoying or upsetting (e.g. outside someone's house)
- using rude, abusive or insulting language
- threatening behaviour or bullying, including on the internet or via mobile phone
- being racist or homophobic towards others
- owning uncontrolled or dangerous dogs
- joyriding or using vehicles in an anti-social manner (e.g. blocking access, playing loud music, wheel spinning)
- drinking alcohol to excess, causing alcohol-related trouble or buying and selling drugs.

Why do you think anti-social behaviour can be so distressing to many members of the public?

The impact of anti-social behaviour can be terrible, both for communities and individuals. People may feel that their neighbours do not look out for one another and community spirit is weakened. Anti-social behaviour has even driven people to commit suicide.

There are many things the services can do to reduce or control anti-social behaviour, such as issuing anti-social behaviour orders (ASBOs), using warning letters and contracts of behaviour, issuing eviction notices against anti-social neighbours and issuing parenting orders.

Activity 4.1	Anti-social behaviour

Research the case of Fiona Pilkington and her daughter Francecca using the internet. Ms Pilkington killed herself and her daughter in October 2007 after years of abuse and targeted anti-social behaviour. Using your research, answer the following questions.

1 How did the police respond to Ms Pilkington's complaints?

2 What more could have been done by the services to support the Pilkingtons?

3 How can the services, working in partnership with the community, stop or prevent anti-social behaviour?

▶ Virtual communities

Virtual communities have grown over the last 20 years as social media and online gaming have become more popular. Popular social media sites where information can be exchanged and relationships formed include:

- Facebook
- Twitter
- Snapchat
- Tumblr
- Kik
- Vine
- Instagram
- Pheed.

These social media platforms have different focuses. Some concentrate on video sharing, while others focus on text or photos. However, what they all have in common is the ability to share thoughts instantaneously with hundreds of other people and to create online 'friends' or 'followers' as part of a wider online community.

Online games are another forum in which people make friends and build communities. These might include games such as *World of Warcraft* or *Call of Duty*, which encourage individuals to band together in groups to fight enemies and achieve objectives.

Virtual communities can be a lifeline for many people who are not able to leave their home or who do not have the confidence to interact with people directly. Virtual communities have to be protected from a range of online threats, such as fraud and potential child abuse.

Discussion

Most people belong to at least one online community. Which online communities do you belong to? How does being a member of this community improve your quality of life?

Did you know?

Paedophiles have been known to contact young people through social media sites by pretending to be another young person.

Remember

- Do not post any personal information online and be careful when posting pictures of yourself.
- Do not be rude or say anything online that you would not say in person.
- Do not meet up with people you have met online.
- Do not give out your password.
- Remember that not everyone online is who they say they are.
- If you feel uncomfortable with someone's online behaviour, tell a tutor or parent.

Key term

Homophobia – an extreme and irrational dislike of homosexuality or homosexuals.

Discussion

Did you know that information you upload about yourself to many virtual communities is available for future employers to see? How would you feel if the recruiting officer for your chosen service looked at your Facebook posts and photographs? Would you be embarrassed or upset about this?

Protection from fraud and identity crime

It is not unusual for people to have their Facebook accounts or gaming accounts hacked. This can lead to criminals getting hold of their personal data and stealing their identity. As a result, many social media and gaming companies spend a lot of time and money ensuring that online accounts are secure, particularly any personal or financial details.

Child protection

In any online community, children's safety can also be at risk. Not everyone on social media is who they say they are, and it is important that you never give out personal information like your address that could lead to your identification.

Case study

In 2013, 17-year-old Paris Brown was appointed as the UK's first Youth Police and Crime Commissioner in Kent with an annual salary of £15,000. She resigned just six days after starting the job, when it came to light that tweets she had posted between the ages of 14 and 16 could have been considered racist and **homophobic**.

1 Why do you think Paris chose to resign from this position?

2 Do you think people should be held to account for posts on social media which they made as children?

3 Is there anything on your social media profile(s) which might cost you a job or change an employer's opinion of you? If so, what can you do about it?

▶ Cultural and religious communities

A cultural community is formed when people with similar backgrounds, values, behaviours or beliefs gather together or live close to each other. For example, cultural communities often form when people move to a different country. People feel comfortable when they are with others who speak their language and understand their culture, and when they move abroad they often like to be with people from the same background for this reason. Good examples of this include:

- Little Germany in Bradford – in the mid and late 1800s, many German merchants were drawn to Bradford by the textile industry and settled in one area of the city
- the Costa del Sol region of southern Spain – up to 300,000 Britons live for some or all of the year in and around the Costa del Sol.

A religious community is made up of people who share a faith or spiritual way of life. They normally centre around a place of worship, such as a church or mosque, where people can gather to practise their religion and socialise with others of the same faith. Places of worship can be at the heart of creating a community spirit.

Freedom from intolerance and freedom to worship

Cultural and religious communities need to be protected from hostility to their way of life. Freedom to worship means that everyone has the freedom to worship without harassment. Similarly, an individual's cultural background should not put them at risk of harm.

Intolerance often comes about because of a lack of understanding. The public services can have a role in educating people to prevent intolerance as well as in protecting specific religious and cultural communities. This is why you may find the public services delivering community education in schools, youth centres and religious venues such as mosques.

 # Ethnic communities

As with cultural and religious communities, ethnic communities consist of people who spend time with people of the same or similar ethnic background. Having the same ethnic background as someone else might also mean that you share their culture and religion.

Protection from prejudice and ethnic abuse

Ethnic communities need protection from prejudice and ethnic abuse. In 2013, there were almost 50,000 racist incidents of crime. A crime is classed as rascist if it is perceived by the victim or any other person to be motivated by hostility or prejudice based on the victim's race.

Age-based communities

Age-based communities are formed when individuals group together with others based on their age, such as teenagers or the elderly. People tend to have a lot in common with other people of the same age. They are likely to have experienced similar things, to be familiar with the same popular culture, to be at the same stage in life or to enjoy similar activities. Age-based communities can be found in places such as halls of residence at universities, retirement homes, community centres and youth clubs.

Age-based communities experience different types of risks and therefore need different types of protection against different things.

Protection from child abuse, drug abuse and the effects of age

Younger people are more at risk of gang- and drug-related activity, and they are more vulnerable online. Older people are generally more at risk of confidence crimes, such as being forced into unnecessary building work by unscrupulous door-to-door builders or having thieves trick their way into homes using fake identification.

Both groups are also vulnerable to the risk of abuse by family members. For younger people, this might be emotional, physical or sexual abuse. For older people, it might be financial or physical abuse, and could include neglect.

Did you know?

Britain has not always allowed people freedom of worship. During the seventeenth century, religious groups such as the Baptists and the Religious Society of Friends (Quakers) were persecuted for their beliefs. Many emigrated because of this persecution.

Activity 4.2   Different types of protection

Drug dealers are unlikely to target an old people's residential home, but they do target secondary schools and colleges.

Why is there a difference in the types of protection needed by different communities?

▶ How the public services serve the needs of particular communities

Introduction

The public services have to offer the right levels of service to each type of community. This means ensuring that the right service and personnel are deployed at the right time, which can be quite a challenge. How do you think the services know what to do and when? How much contact do they have with the communities they serve?

There are several types of public service, including:

- emergency services (blue light services)
- armed services
- local authorities
- central government
- voluntary services (third sector services).

These groups work to protect all communities. Where required, they will focus their work specifically on the needs of individual communities in order to protect the people and interests within them.

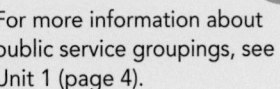

Link

For more information about public service groupings, see Unit 1 (page 4).

▶ Emergency services

The main emergency services are the Police, Fire and Rescue and Ambulance Services and are usually contacted by calling 999. However, in some parts of the country the emergency services can also include HM Coastguard, Mountain Rescue and Cave Rescue. Each emergency service serves and protects particular communities in different ways.

The Police Service

The Police Service does many things to serve and protect its communities. For example, it introduced community policing to give local communities a greater say about the way their area is policed. The Police Service has also increased the number of special constables and police community support officers (PCSOs) to tackle anti-social behaviour and low-level crime. This allows regular police officers to concentrate on more serious crimes while still taking action to protect communities against anti-social behaviour.

The Police Service also works hard to protect communities by educating people about crime prevention. This includes keeping themselves and their property safe. They educate children on how to avoid becoming involved in crime. They do this by visiting schools and discussing drugs awareness, the consequences of criminal behaviour and the impact of gang-related activity on families and individuals.

The police also keep large-scale community events safe, such as football matches and other sporting or cultural events. They provide specific advice to sections of the community that may be targeted by hate crime or criminals, such as ethnic or religious minorities and the elderly.

The Fire and Rescue Service

The main role of the Fire and Rescue Service in protecting local communities is to put out fires. However, they also provide other fire prevention services to the community, such as fire safety advice in schools and businesses, and advice on fire alarm choice and fire alarm fitting for households and businesses. This can be especially useful for members of the community who may not be able to fit smoke alarms for themselves, such as the elderly.

Fire and Rescue Services also work with young people in schools and in extracurricular youth activities. These activities are designed to prevent young people becoming involved in fire-related crime or being harmed in accidental fires. In many communities, this includes a Community Fire Cadets programme. Cadets learn about the Fire and Rescue Service and get a feel for the job that firefighters do.

Some Fire and Rescue Services also try to assist with crime reduction by providing activities for young people, such as boxing clubs, to divert them away from crime.

The Ambulance Service

Primarily, the Ambulance Service protects communities by responding to 999 calls and treating casualties at the scene of an incident. However, they also offer passenger transport services to take the elderly or individuals with disabilities to hospital appointments. This puts these more vulnerable members of society at lower risk than if they had to rely on public transport.

Just checking

1 List three different types of community.
2 Describe one type of community in detail.
3 Explain how the emergency services protect local communities.
4 Explain how the Police Service protects one particular community.

▶ Armed services

The armed services protect the interests of the UK in conflict situations and on peacekeeping missions. They include the British Army, the Royal Navy and the Royal Air Force (RAF).

The British Army

The British Army not only works overseas in conflict or peacekeeping situations but also protects communities in the UK. Most commonly, they offer assistance to the emergency services in times of severe weather or flooding, to evacuate communities and protect the public's property. For example, in September 2012, soldiers from the 2nd Signal Regiment helped to fill and lay thousands of sandbags in York city centre to defend against flooding.

The British Army also runs the Army Cadet Force for young people. This teaches young people discipline, confidence and teamworking skills, and prepares them for a life in the services. It can also help to divert young people away from anti-social behaviour by teaching them discipline and respect.

The Royal Navy

Like the British Army, the Royal Navy runs cadet forces for young people, which teach them discipline, respect and the importance of teamwork.

The Royal Navy runs community centres on or near naval bases, to help families cope with the difficulties caused by loved ones being away from home on naval tours of duty. These centres offer community education and activities as well as personal and family support. They may also be open to local non-services families.

The Royal Navy also helps to prevent illegal drug smuggling all over the world. While this might not seem to have much of an impact on communities in the UK, every shipment of drugs seized is one fewer that can be sold in local communities in the UK. This reduces drug abuse and associated crimes.

The Royal Air Force (RAF)

Like the British Army and the Royal Navy, the RAF runs the Air Cadets programme for young people, which has the same benefits for the local community as the other cadet forces listed above.

The RAF also works with volunteer agencies like Mountain Rescue to airlift injured walkers and climbers to safety, and to provide a search and rescue service at sea. Like the Royal Navy, the RAF also offers community services to the families of service personnel.

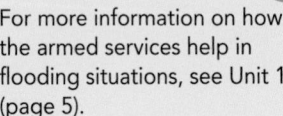

Link

For more information on how the armed services help in flooding situations, see Unit 1 (page 5).

How do the armed services support other public services during major incidents or severe weather events?

Local and central government

Local and central government services cover a wide range of activities that protect and support local communities. These activities include emergency planning as well as education, health and leisure services.

Emergency planning

Emergency planning is led by local government and it covers emergencies which are too large or complex for each public service to deal with individually. It plans to coordinate all the activities of the services to protect communities against large-scale emergency incidents. These can include rail crashes, terrorist attacks, floods, chemical spillages or large-scale fires.

The local authority also works with voluntary agencies to prepare for emergency situations.

Education services

Education is a less obvious way of protecting a community, but it is just as important as other activities such as health and leisure services. Young people who have an education and who can see the value of education are less likely to be involved in crime and disorder, and more likely to support their families and communities.

Education can protect young people from dangerous situations by advising them on personal and online safety, and on what to do if they are in trouble and need help.

Education can protect older people from becoming victims of crime by making them aware of scams in the local area. It can also keep them healthier and more active.

Local authorities and local schools and colleges provide education for children and adults who have English as their second language. This helps them to get work, to do better in their studies and to integrate into local communities.

Health services

Health care services protect communities by providing treatment for injuries and illnesses. They also educate people about lifestyle choices such as smoking, drinking or taking drugs.

Health care workers have to serve the needs of local communities by respecting the cultural or religious needs of their patients. This could include ensuring that some patients are treated by members of the same sex, or given different food because of religious dietary requirements, such as **halal** or **kosher** food.

Leisure services

Leisure services include facilities such as community centres, sports centres, swimming baths and libraries. Leisure services protect the community by improving health and fitness and by providing opportunities for people to meet others and avoid loneliness.

It is important that individuals with disabilities and the elderly are not disadvantaged by a lack of access to leisure facilities. This may mean that the local authority needs to provide access equipment, such as lifts or hoists in swimming pools and access ramps in public buildings.

 Key terms

Halal – a halal diet abides by the principles of Islam and does not include alcohol, pork or pork products. Animals killed for meat must be killed in a particular way.

Kosher – a kosher diet abides by the principles of Judaism and does not include pork and pork products. Meat and dairy food should not be eaten together, and animals killed for meat must be killed in a particular way.

Activity 4.3　Protecting communities

The services provide a wide range of support and protection to local communities. Produce a poster which could be displayed in local facilities which includes the following information.

1　Provide a list of how the emergency and armed services protect the local community.

2　Identify how the local authority helps people with disabilities and the elderly.

3　Explain how education can reduce crime and disorder.

Voluntary services

Voluntary services often provide services that neither the public nor the private sector can, which is why they are sometimes called the third sector. They usually rely on donations by businesses and individuals to do their work. They address a wide range of issues, such as housing and homelessness, maritime emergencies and protection of the vulnerable or marginalised.

Shelter

Shelter is a charity which focuses on providing good quality, affordable housing and working to combat homelessness. It was established in 1966 and gets over 50% of its income from donations by members of the public and businesses. Shelter also employs more than 1,000 people nationally.

Shelter supports and protects communities who struggle with poor or inadequate living conditions, as well as the homeless community. It protects people from bad landlords and supports tenants in disputes with landlords over issues such as unlawful evictions. It also campaigns for better tenants' rights.

Did you know?

In November 2013, government figures showed that around 80,000 children were homeless and living in emergency accommodation.

The Royal National Lifeboat Institution (RNLI)

The RNLI provides 24-hour search and rescue services around the coast of the UK, as well as beach lifeguard services. The RNLI was founded in 1824 and has saved more than 140,000 lives since then. It rescues an average of 23 people every day. It also has a flood rescue team available 24 hours a day, who are specifically trained to conduct search and rescue in fast moving water.

Salvation Army

The Salvation Army is a Christian church and a registered charity which offers a wide range of services to help and protect people who are vulnerable or marginalised. The church has around 50,000 members and about 4,000 employees.

The Salvation Army sometimes supports the emergency services, as its community centres can be used as shelter for people who have been evacuated from their homes. As part of this, it provides on-site refreshments to emergency service responders and civilians.

The Salvation Army provides a wide range of services, some of which are shown in Figure 4.2.

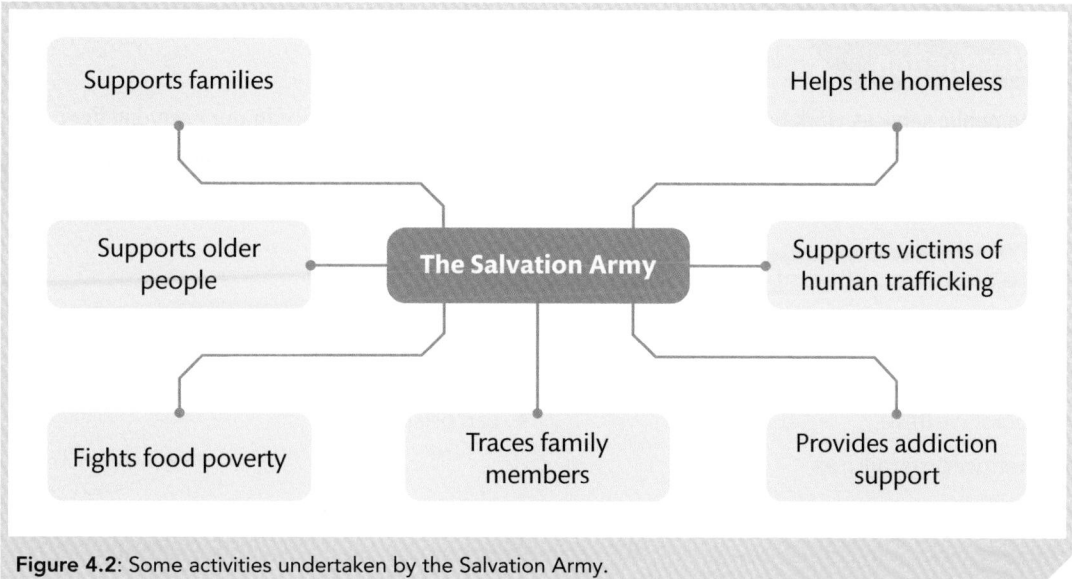

Figure 4.2: Some activities undertaken by the Salvation Army.

Assessment activity 4.1

You are a feature writer for your local college newspaper. You have been asked to write a 'community news' page about the essential role played by the public services in protecting the local community. You have been asked because the services need to build good relationships with young people in your college.

As part of the article you should discuss the different types of communities and consider how different services support the communities with which they work.

Tips

- When writing your article, consider the advantages to the community of services working together to protect them.
- It may also be useful to examine how different services do different things to protect the same communities.

▶ Hazards and risks

Introduction

The public services work hard to protect us and manage the risks we face in our everyday lives. Do you know what the most common risks to your community are? Can you think how the services might work together to achieve their goal and keep us safe?

Key terms 🔑

Hazard – a potential source of harm to a person or group of people.

Risk – the likelihood that a person or group of people may be harmed by a hazard.

There are many different kinds of **hazards** and **risks**, including:

- natural disasters
- human activity
- social welfare
- technology failures
- human errors
- environmental hazards
- terrorism.

It is important to remember that risk is a natural part of life. By carefully managing hazards, risks can be reduced, but they cannot be eliminated. This means that, sometimes, incidents cannot be prevented. In these cases, the public services deal with the aftermath of the incident.

How can the services manage large-scale natural disasters?

▶ Natural disasters

Natural disasters are not a very common hazard in the UK but they are common in some other parts of the world. Natural disasters include:

- earthquakes
- mudslides
- floods
- volcanoes
- hurricanes
- tornadoes
- drought and famine
- forest fires
- disease epidemics.

Natural disasters can kill many individuals and devastate whole communities. Often the risk posed by natural disasters cannot be reduced, and all that the public services can do is try to rescue as many people as they can after the event. Examples of natural disasters include:

- 2013 – Typhoon Haiyan – caused massive destruction in the Philippines and the loss of over 5,000 lives
- 2011 – Japanese tsunami – killed over 15,000 people and caused a system failure at a nuclear power plant, as well as destroying many towns and villages.

Human activity

Crime and anti-social behaviour are two of the most common hazards in the UK. The Office for National Statistics estimated that between September 2012 and September 2013, 8 million crimes were committed against households and adults, and 859,000 crimes were committed against children aged 10–15. These included:

- nearly 60,000 sexual crimes
- over 600,000 incidents of violence against people
- 1.8 million instances of theft.

The public services work hard to reduce the risks of crime and anti-social behaviour for individuals and communities by educating people about how to keep themselves and their property safe. They use CCTV to catch criminals and prevent crime, and remove problem tenants from areas where they are known to cause trouble. They also provide youth services such as clubs which help to keep young people out of trouble.

Social welfare

It is important to use social welfare and the public services to protect vulnerable groups from cruelty and harassment. Groups in the UK whose welfare is particularly at risk include children, the elderly and individuals with learning difficulties or disabilities. The services can manage these risks by providing social workers and support workers such as home helpers, specialist mental health professionals and special needs teachers.

Vulnerable sections of society may also be affected by poverty. Up to 3.5 million children in the UK live in poverty, while 1.2 million pensioners live on low incomes.

It is also thought that people with disabilities are significantly more likely to be victims of crime than other people. Research by the charity Mencap suggested that 90% of people with learning difficulties have been bullied or harassed because of their disability.

The most effective ways in which the public services can protect these vulnerable groups are:

- educating individuals, groups and communities about the impact and consequences of discrimination, as a preventative measure
- ensuring that vulnerable members of society know who to contact if they need help and support.

Did you know?

Nearly one in five people in the UK have a disability.

Discussion

What can the public services do to help the most vulnerable groups in our society and protect them from hazards and risks? Discuss this with your classmates and make a list of possible actions.

Technology failures or human error

Technology failures are failures of equipment or structures, often due to their age, overuse or lack of maintenance. Examples of technological causes of incidents include:

- metal fatigue or other wear
- faulty wiring
- design faults
- extreme physical stress with which the technology was not designed to cope
- insufficient maintenance
- equipment failure
- the use of inappropriate equipment.

Human causes of hazards and risks include mistakes or deliberate acts of sabotage. Examples of human causes include:

- pilot or driver error
- acts of terrorism
- intoxication
- sabotage
- speeding
- incompetence.

Major rail, road and air accidents with identified human causes occur all over the world. For example, in July 2013, a train crash in northern Spain which killed 79 people appears to have been caused by driver error and excessive speed.

▶ Environmental hazards

There are many environmental hazards and risks from which the public services work hard to protect us, including:

- fly tipping
- food safety
- pollution
- chemical waste disposal.

Public services are constantly working on our behalf to ensure that the food we eat, the water we drink and the environment we live in are as clean as possible. This means that they take responsibility for refuse collection and recycling, for making sure food sold in shops and restaurants is fit for purpose and is actually what it says it is, and for monitoring and reducing pollution. They also ensure that companies and individuals dispose of chemicals safely, rather than pouring them down the drain or dumping them.

▶ Terrorism

The UK has been subject to a number of terrorist attacks over the last 50 years. Some of these were as a result of conflict in Northern Ireland, including the Enniskillen bombing in 1987, which killed 11 people, and the Warrington bombing in 1993, which killed two people. Terrorist attacks in the UK have also been perpetrated by Islamic extremists, such as the 7/7 London bombings in 2005, which killed 52 people.

The public services work very hard to share information on potential terrorist threats and to remove those threats before they become a reality. However, acting to protect the community can also put members of the public services in harm's way.

Case study

In May 2013, Michael Adebolajo, 29, and Michael Adebowale, 22, murdered soldier Lee Rigby, 25, outside Woolwich barracks in south London. The brutal attack was witnessed by many people and video footage of the aftermath of the attack was posted online. The two men apparently killed Drummer Rigby in revenge for the deaths of Muslims overseas as a result of British foreign policy. They were found guilty of murder.

1 What can the public services do to protect the community from extremists?

2 How can the public services share information effectively on terrorist threats?

3 How can they work with different communities to remove the risk of extremism?

Risk avoidance

It is better to avoid risks entirely where possible than to have to deal with an incident once harm has occurred. Risks can be avoided through contingency planning and risk assessment.

Contingency or emergency planning

Contingency planning means planning for a situation which is not covered by everyday working plans. It is a professional way of saying 'plan B'. It is designed to minimise the impact of an emergency event and ensure that communities and businesses can get back to normal as soon as possible.

Contingency planning assumes that anything that can go wrong will go wrong, and puts a plan in place to deal with it. This could include filling sandbags, digging ditches and preparing an evacuation plan when there is a high risk of flooding.

In order to build a contingency plan, you have to know the hazards and risks of a particular situation. You then decide which risks must be dealt with as a priority by considering their likely impact. This is called a risk assessment.

Risk assessments normally have five stages that you work through in order to identify the range of risks:

1 What are the hazards?

2 Who might be harmed and how?

3 What are you already doing to prevent the hazard from hurting anyone?

4 Do you need to do anything else to control the risk?

5 Who needs to take action to control the risk?

As a result of your risk assessment, you can then put control measures in place. These are actions designed to reduce the level of risk posed by a hazard or remove it entirely.

Remember

A **hazard** is a potential source of harm or injury, such as a broken step or water on the floor.

A **risk** is the likelihood that a person might be harmed by exposure to a hazard.

Control measures are the actions that you can take to remove the hazard or reduce the likelihood that someone will be harmed by exposure to the hazard.

		Potential severity of harm		
		Slightly harmful	**Harmful**	**Extremely harmful**
Likelihood of harm occurring	**Highly unlikely**	Insignificant risk	Low risk	Medium risk
	Unlikely	Low risk	Medium risk	High risk
	Likely	Medium risk	High risk	Extreme risk

Figure 4.3: A risk matrix. This can be used to decide which risks are highest and should be tackled first.

Activity 4.4　Managing risk

You have been working with the public services as a cadet and have been advised that heavy rainfall and strong winds are predicted. A flood warning is in place on the local river. In the centre of your village, there is a residential home for elderly people and a children's day nursery. Your team of cadets has been asked to work with the residential home and the day nursery to prepare for the bad weather.

Consider the five stages of risk assessment and answer the questions below.

1　What are the hazards?

2　Who is at risk?

3　What can you and your cadet team do to control the risks?

Control measures should always be considered in the order in which they are listed in Table 4.1.

Table 4.1: Control measures.

Control measure	Description
Elimination	• Remove or avoid the risk altogether by getting rid of the hazard. • Could include scrapping a dangerous machine and replacing it, or wiping up water on the floor so that no one slips. • Not all risks can be eliminated. For example, you cannot get rid of an earthquake or a severe storm. In these cases you have to find other ways of minimising the risk.
Substitution	• Replace a hazard with a less dangerous one. Allows you to do the job you need to do, but in safer conditions. • Could include changing an expedition route to avoid high climbs and unstable ground. • Some hazards cannot be substituted so you may have to find other ways of controlling the risks.
Control the risk at its source	• Manage hazards at their source rather than waiting for the risk to become widespread. • Could include using a remote controlled robot to enter hazardous buildings rather than risking a person's life, or placing hand guards on dangerous machinery. • Controlling the hazard at the source does not change the hazard. It just keeps it away from the people who might get hurt by it.
Education and training	• Change the way people work by educating or training them to work safely, ensuring procedures are followed and safety signs and notices are present. • Could include not eating or drinking in laboratories, training staff to do their own risk assessments and making sure they have all had health and safety training.
Personal protective equipment (PPE)	• Should be provided free of charge by your employer. • Could include helmets, stab vests, earplugs in a noisy environment or gloves to prevent infection in a medical environment. • Last resort only. There should always be other control measures in place, not just PPE.

Risk avoidance at work

People in the public services encounter many hazards as part of their working day, and they have to deal with these hazards in order to do their job and deliver the service the public needs. Common hazards in the public services include:

- angry members of the public
- criminal activity
- fires
- chemical spillages
- infection.

The services spend a lot of time and money trying to eliminate the risks to their own staff, communities and the general public. Spending time and money on incident prevention is often far more cost effective than dealing with an incident after it has happened. The services also assist factories and manufacturing companies to avoid potential incidents and help them develop action plans to ensure incidents are not repeated.

Did you know?

The key government body responsible for health and safety in the workplace is the Health and Safety Executive (HSE). You can use their website for research.

Discussion

The public services are risky professions. Uniformed and non-uniformed staff will encounter a variety of different hazards throughout their working day. How can they as individuals protect themselves and control these risks while at work? Discuss this with your classmates and note your main points.

You spend a lot of time at work and have the right to be safe at work. The Health and Safety Executive's annual figures for 2012/13 on health and safety in the workplace showed that:

- 148 workers were killed at work
- 1.1 million people suffered from a work-related illness
- 27 million working days were lost because of work-related illness and injury.

That is why employers and employees have a legal obligation to follow safe working practices and report injuries.

Activity 4.5   Control measures

Using the control measures in Table 4.1, consider what the public services could do to manage the following risks. Remember to start with elimination and work down to PPE.

1 Sending a soldier to serve as part of the ISAF in Afghanistan.
2 A firefighter responding to a road traffic incident.
3 A housing worker dealing with an aggressive tenant.
4 A charity worker operating a mobile food kitchen for the homeless at night.

▶ Individual involvement in community protection

Introduction

Protecting the communities in which we live is not just the responsibility of the public services. It is a responsibility for all of us. What would the area you live in be like if everyone took responsibility for how it looked and how safe it was? What do you do to look after and protect your community? Is there more you could do?

Key term

Stereotypes – widely held views which present an oversimplified or generalised opinion.

▶ Young people

There is a **stereotype** that young people are not concerned about their community and cause trouble in their local area. However, there is no evidence to suggest that young people cause problems in communities more than any other group. In fact, many young people are actively involved in supporting their communities. For example:

- the armed services have over 130,000 cadets
- over half of St John Ambulance volunteers are under 25
- there are many police cadets and youth fire service volunteers.

Young people in cadet forces often support their communities by doing volunteer work or fundraising. They also prepare themselves to give better support in the future, by learning about teamwork, discipline and problem solving. Many cadets also have the opportunity to complete qualifications as part of their training.

Young people do not have to join a cadet service to give something back to the community. They may check on elderly neighbours, run coaching activities for younger children in school holidays, or even act as young carers to family members with disabilities.

Did you know?

There are 178,000 young carers in England and Wales. The average age of a young carer is 12, but some children care for disabled family members from the age of 5.

What are the benefits of joining the cadets?

Many young people also have an active role in raising money for local and national charities such as Race for Life, Children in Need or Red Nose Day, as well as local facilities such as hospices and special care baby units.

▶ Action groups

Action groups are groups of people who protect their local community. They include groups such as Neighbourhood Watch, Speed Watch and Farm Watch.

Neighbourhood Watch is considered to be one of the largest and most successful crime prevention initiatives ever introduced. Members get together with their neighbours to monitor their local area and report anything suspicious to the police.

Neighbourhood Watch schemes are not just about cutting the rates of burglary and theft in an area. They also have other positive effects, such as:

- reducing fear of crime
- building stronger communities
- helping people get to know their neighbours
- reducing other types of crime
- building positive relationships with the police.

The success of Neighbourhood Watch has led to other similar schemes such as Speed Watch and Farm Watch. Farm Watch allows farmers and landowners to work with each other and the police to prevent rural crime and protect farms.

Discussion

What have you done to support and protect your community recently? Do you raise money for charity? Or are you a cadet? Discuss these questions with your classmates and consider what else you can do in your community.

Case study

Since the 1970s, some fertilisers have been used by terrorist groups as an ingredient in homemade explosives. These explosives use a chemical called ammonium nitrate, which is found in agricultural fertilisers. For example, the Oklahoma Bombing in the USA was caused by American terrorists using a bomb made from fertilisers.

The UK currently manufactures or imports about 4 million tonnes of ammonium nitrate and ammonium nitrate-based fertilisers each year. In September 2013, 62 tons of ammonium nitrate were stolen from a farm in Lincolnshire. Many countries have banned the use of ammonium nitrate, including Germany, China and Afghanistan.

1 Why is it important that farmers and people who live in rural areas support and protect their communities?

2 What are the dangers of leaving ammonium nitrate-based fertilisers unsecured?

3 Do you think we should continue to use ammonium nitrate-based fertilisers?

The Speed Watch scheme is used in communities where residents are concerned about the speed of traffic. It gives local communities the chance to get actively involved in monitoring the speed of vehicles travelling through their neighbourhood. Speeding cars can affect the well-being of communities, particularly if they are a problem outside schools or near children's play areas.

Child protection

Individuals have an important role to play in the protection of young people and children in local communities. Many children in the UK experience abuse at the hands of their families or other members of their community. In 2012, over 40,000 children in England were the subject of a child protection plan because they were at risk of physical, emotional or sexual abuse.

Many children are also bullied at school. The NSPCC believes that almost half of children are bullied at some point in their time at school.

Individuals can work to protect children by reporting abuse if they suspect it is happening. They can also cooperate with child protection agencies such as the Police Service, social services and charities such as the NSPCC or Save the Children.

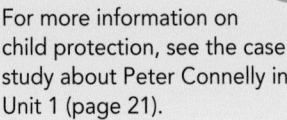

Link

For more information on child protection, see the case study about Peter Connelly in Unit 1 (page 21).

Special constabulary

Special constables or 'specials' are part-time police volunteers. They are ordinary members of the community who give up at least four hours per week to support the Police Service. Their uniform is similar to that worn by the police and they have the same powers as regular officers.

Special constables form a vital link between the police and the local community and enable ordinary citizens, many of whom do different day jobs, to directly support and protect their local community.

Did you know?

There are around 19,000 special constables working alongside their full-time colleagues in England and Wales.

Youth offending teams

Youth offending teams (YOTs) work with young people who have been in trouble with the police or who are at serious risk of offending. These teams are part of the local council and they work with a variety of different organisations such as:

- the Police Service
- probation officers
- health, housing and children's services
- schools and education authorities
- charities and the local community.

They try to keep young people away from crime and help them understand the impact of their behaviour on their victims and on their own families. They use a multi-agency approach to provide the services that young offenders need to help turn them away from crime.

Magistrates

Magistrates are unpaid volunteers who are trained to serve as representatives of their local community. They sit in panels of three and have a trained legal advisor on hand at all times when in court. Even though they are volunteers, they must commit to a minimum number of days in order to be able to fulfil their role, which in 2014 is a minimum of 13 days or 26 half days.

As they are not legally trained, magistrates do not deal with complex or difficult cases. Instead they **try** low-level criminal offences in the magistrates' court and the youth court, and refer more serious cases to the Crown Court which has the power to deal with them.

Magistrates are often referred to as the backbone of the criminal justice system as they deal with around 97% of all criminal cases. It is important to remember that magistrates are unpaid volunteers taken directly from the local community – they serve the community and the criminal justice system for reasons other than money.

Key term

Try – to put someone on trial.

Activity 4.6   Personal characteristics

List and describe five personal characteristics that you think would be useful if you wanted to become a magistrate. How do these characteristics compare with the characteristics needed in other public service roles?

Protecting the environment

Recycling is the process of taking old and used materials such as plastic or glass and using them to create new products. Many things can be recycled, including paper, metal, plastic and clothing.

Recycling has many benefits for the community including:

- protecting the environment
- saving energy
- reducing landfill
- protecting the supply of raw materials.

Local councils in the UK now provide a doorstep recycling service. Most households have different bins into which they can put different materials. By recycling you can reduce air and ground pollution and therefore help your local community stay healthy.

Activity 4.7   Recycling

England alone generates about 177 million tonnes of waste every year. This is a poor use of resources and costs businesses and households money. It also causes environmental damage – for example, waste sent to landfill produces methane, a powerful greenhouse gas.

Produce some posters about the importance of recycling. These could be for your school or college or another facility in your local community.

▶ Types of multi-agency working

Introduction

Multi-agency work is when a number of services come together to achieve an objective. When facing risks and hazards it often pays to be part of a bigger team, with more personnel, resources and expertise. Why do you think this is? What are the advantages of multi-agency working?

The services often work together on a number of local, regional, national and even international risks and hazards. Some of the most common situations where a multi-agency approach might be adopted include natural disasters and safety campaigns on a variety of different topics.

▶ Natural disasters

Natural disasters, such as mudslides and floods, always require a multi-agency response. There are often so many people and so many properties at risk that it is impossible for one service to do everything. The UK is more likely to be affected by flooding than by other natural disasters, such as earthquakes, volcanoes or tsunamis.

In a flood situation the following services may be involved:

- the Police Service
- the Fire and Rescue Service
- the local authority
- the RNLI
- the Salvation Army and other charities
- the Department for the Environment, Food and Rural Affairs (Defra).

These groups would work together to:

- evacuate the public from the area at risk
- reinforce flood defences such as sandbags
- operate emergency shelters
- provide food to evacuees.

▶ Health issues

Health issues such as smoking, drinking and obesity cost the NHS billions of pounds every year. They also cost people their health and even their lives. It takes many services to come together to create a campaign that can change the behaviour of so many individuals.

A good example of the services working together in this way would be for a national anti-smoking campaign, where the following services might come together:

- the Department of Health
- local authorities
- the NHS
- schools
- anti-smoking charities such as Action on Smoking and Health (ASH).

Road safety

In 2012, 1,754 people were killed in road accidents in the UK, and just over 23,000 people were seriously injured. Many road traffic incidents require the response of several different services working together to rescue and treat the injured and protect the scene.

Reducing the hazards and risks associated with roads requires the teamwork of many of the public services, such as:

- the Police, Fire and Rescue, and Ambulance Services
- Department for Transport
- schools and colleges
- local authorities
- local residents involved in Speed Watch
- charities such as the Royal Society for the Prevention of Accidents (RoSPA) and Brake (a road safety charity).

These agencies work together to:

- improve roads
- increase awareness of hazardous behaviour such as drink driving and texting while driving
- campaign for and support changes in the law
- offer remedial training for drivers who have been caught driving in a hazardous manner.

Take it further

Do some research into current or previous road safety campaigns. Find out how the services ensure that their information reaches people.

Activity 4.8 Multi-agency work

Consider a problem in your local community such as littering or fly-tipping. Draw up a plan to combat the problem which:

- identifies the impact of the problem
- lists the services that might be involved
- describes how the community and services could work together to improve the situation.

Safeguarding children

Many children are the victims of violence, sexual crime and bullying. It is essential to reduce these risks and to make children aware of what to do if they have been a victim. Safety campaigns include the NSPCC's Full Stop Campaign, which brought together a number of services to end violence against children, including:

- the Police Service
- education services
- social services
- health services.

The primary goal of the services working together in this way is to raise awareness of the seriousness of violence against children and to help professionals recognise the signs of abuse in order to report it. A multi-agency approach also supports parents or other abusers seeking help to stop their violent behaviour as well as providing a safe environment in which children can report and discuss abuse.

Local community action

Anti-social behaviour and crime can ruin local communities. They can also turn families and individuals away from the community so that they only look after themselves and their loved ones.

If multi-agency work is to be successful in reducing crime and anti-social behaviour, the community and the individuals in it need to be part of the team that deals with these problems. These teams can involve:

- action groups such as Neighbourhood Watch and Speed Watch
- volunteer programmes such as Neighbourhood Improvement Volunteers and special constables
- the Police Service
- community safety partnerships
- churches and other faith groups
- charities such as Stonewall
- local authorities.

Take it further

Find out what action groups and volunteer programmes are in place in your local community.

Assessment activity 4.2

Your college has very good relationships with several local schools. Your tutor would like to give pupils in these schools information on how the public services protect communities. This will help the pupils to improve their knowledge and help the public services to strengthen community relationships.

As part of this, you have been asked to:

- produce an information booklet which can be given to the pupils
- make a short presentation to be used by teachers.

When you compile your information, make sure you show how communities manage risks and hazards, and explain the benefits of contingency planning. You will also need to discuss the impact of multi-agency work, as well as ways in which public services can be supported by individuals.

Tips

- Consider all of the elements that are included in risk management such as contingency plans.
- Make sure you discuss the advantages of individual involvement in supporting the services and consider including some examples.
- Give some examples of how the services work together to offer community protection.

WorkSpace

▶ Jason Munroe

Mountain Rescue volunteer

I am a teacher at a local school, but I also volunteer with the local Mountain Rescue unit. This means taking my mobile phone into class in case I have to attend a call-out. Fortunately the head teacher is also part of the Mountain Rescue team so this doesn't cause me many problems at work.

The local community is very supportive of the Mountain Rescue team, and the team is great to work with: we all pull together and rely on each other when there is a call-out. We can get called out for a variety of reasons. Sometimes a person is injured and can't get down from the hills on their own so we go up and assist. At other times a group of walkers might fail to come back on time and we will send up a search and rescue party to find them. And sometimes people head into the mountains with no intention of coming back. This is always the hardest for the team as we know we are not likely to have a good outcome.

We train and practise regularly, which is great for me because I love spending time hiking and climbing. Best of all, I am glad to have the opportunity to keep my local community and its visitors safe from harm.

Think about it

1 How do volunteers like Jason support the emergency services?
2 How important is it to live locally and know the area in a job like this?
3 Where are your nearest Mountain Rescue centres? How big is the area they cover?

Introduction

Your diet and lifestyle can have a big impact on your fitness levels. Have you ever considered how fit and healthy you might need to be to work in certain public services? Or what sort of fitness tests the different public services might require you to pass?

This unit looks at the effect of nutrition and diet on your health and fitness, and you will examine your own diet and food choices and the impact they may have on your health. It also looks at lifestyle choices such as sexual behaviour, smoking and alcohol consumption and their impact on your well-being.

You will also consider the health and fitness requirements of the public services. You will have the opportunity to try some of the fitness tests for yourself and see what you need to do to improve your performance. This will help you develop an understanding of why you need to take these tests and their relevance to different public service roles.

Assessment: This unit will be assessed through a series of assignments set by your tutor/teacher.

Learning aims

In this unit you will:

A understand the effect of basic nutrition and lifestyle factors on health and fitness

B explore the health and fitness requirements of different public services

C participate in public service fitness tests.

" I've learned lots of things in this unit that will help me improve my diet and fitness. More importantly, I know what fitness levels the services are looking for so I can manage my fitness plan and pass the tests when I apply to the Police Service.

Tadeusz, *15-year-old aspiring police officer* "

Health, Fitness and Lifestyle for the Public Services

5

Assessment Zone

This table shows you what you must do in order to achieve a **Pass**, **Merit** or **Distinction** grade, and where you can find activities to help you.

Assessment criteria			
Level 1	**Level 2 Pass**	**Level 2 Merit**	**Level 2 Distinction**
Learning aim A: Understand the effect of basic nutrition and lifestyle factors on health and fitness			
1A.1 Identify the effects of nutrition on health and fitness.	**2A.P1** Describe the effects of nutrition on health and fitness. **See Assessment activity 5.1, page 151**	**2A.M1** Explain how nutrition and lifestyle factors affect health and fitness. **See Assessment activity 5.1, page 151**	**2A.D1** Analyse the potential impact of nutrition and lifestyle factors on individuals in order to recommend improvements. **See Assessment activity 5.1, page 151**
1A.2 Identify the effects of lifestyle factors on health and fitness.	**2A.P2** Describe the effects of lifestyle factors on health and fitness. **See Assessment activity 5.1, page 151**		
Learning aim B: Explore health and fitness requirements of different public services			
1B.3 List the health and fitness requirements for jobs within three different public services.	**2B.P3** Describe the health and fitness requirements for jobs within three different public services. **See Assessment activity 5.2, page 156**	**2B.M2** Compare the reasons for health and fitness requirements within three public services. **See Assessment activity 5.2, page 156**	**2B.D2** Evaluate the health and fitness requirements within public services with reference to a job role. **See Assessment activity 5.2, page 156**
1B.4 Outline the reasons for the health and fitness requirements within three public services.	**2B.P4** Explain why three public services have health and fitness requirements. **See Assessment activity 5.2, page 156**		
Learning aim C: Be able to take part in public service fitness tests			
1C.5 `Maths` Participate in fitness tests for two contrasting public services, maintaining a results log to identify results.	**2C.P5** `Maths` Participate in fitness tests for two contrasting public services maintaining a results log to describe results. **See Assessment activity 5.3, page 159**	**2C.M3** `Maths` Analyse the results of the fitness tests undertaken for two contrasting public services. **See Assessment activity 5.3, page 159**	**2C.D3** `Maths` Assess the results of the fitness tests undertaken for two contrasting public services to recommend improvements. **See Assessment activity 5.3, page 159**
1C.6 `Maths` Identify the results of fitness tests undertaken for two contrasting public services.	**2C.P6** `Maths` Explain the results of fitness tests undertaken for two contrasting public services. **See Assessment activity 5.3, page 159**		

`Maths`   Opportunity to practise mathematical skills

How you will be assessed

This unit will be assessed by a series of assignments set by your tutor. You will need to explore fitness and nutrition and how it applies to a job in the public services.

You will also assess your own physical performance. You will be expected to demonstrate these skills in practice, and to consider your own performance and what you might need to improve.

Your assessment could be in the form of:

- a logbook
- practical activities
- a report
- a presentation.

▶ Diet and nutrition for a healthy and fit lifestyle

Introduction

If you are considering joining the public services you will need to know about nutrition, lifestyle and health and fitness. This is because many of the services have health and fitness requirements which you must pass in order to get a job with them. Have you thought about your own health or fitness levels? Is your diet healthy or does it require improvement?

Discussion

Do you think you have a healthy diet? How much food do you eat that is high in fat and sugar each day? What could you do to improve your diet?

▶ Basic nutrients

A healthy diet contains a variety of basic nutrients that a body needs for energy, to grow and to stay healthy. These basic nutrients are shown in Figure 5.1.

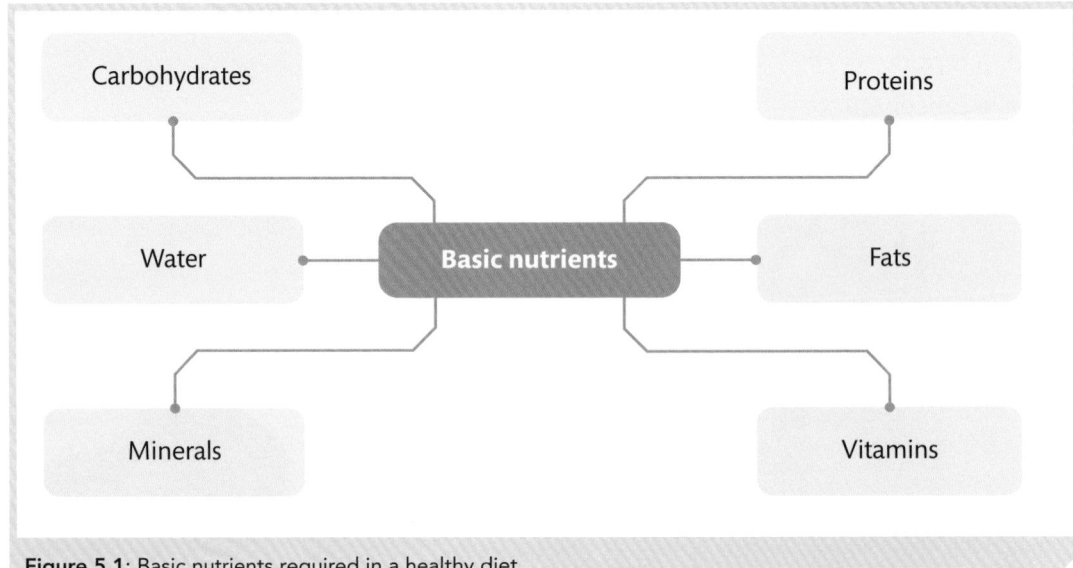

Figure 5.1: Basic nutrients required in a healthy diet.

Did you know?

Your digestive system is made up of the following main organs:

- stomach
- liver
- small intestine
- large intestine
- pancreas and salivary glands.

Carbohydrates

Carbohydrates provide fuel for the body. They are processed by the digestive system and carried in the bloodstream to cells in the body.

There are two main types of carbohydrate:

- **simple carbohydrates** – sugars such as glucose and fructose (found in fruit), which are easily digested and enter the bloodstream quickly
- **complex carbohydrates** – occur when simple carbohydrates bond together to form a chain. Complex carbohydrates are found in foods such as potatoes, cereals, bread, pasta and rice. The digestive system has to break complex carbohydrates into simple carbohydrates in order for them to be absorbed, and as a result they are released into the bloodstream at a much slower pace. This means that they keep you going for longer.

If you have too much sugar in your bloodstream it is stored by the body as a product called glycogen. If there is too much glycogen, it is stored as fat. When you exercise for short periods of time, the glycogen in your liver will be used, but if you exercise for a long time your body will begin to burn fat.

Proteins

Protein is composed of chains of amino acids, which are the building blocks of cells. They provide cells with the materials to grow and maintain their structure. There are two types of amino acids:

- **essential amino acids** – these must be acquired through your food, because your body does not make them for itself, so it is important to have a diet that contains enough of these proteins
- **non-essential amino acids** – these are made for you by your body. They are essential to your **health** and well-being, but they are called non-essential because you do not need to get them from your food.

Protein is found naturally in foods such as meat, fish, milk, eggs and **pulses**.

Fats

We know that a high-fat diet can lead to obesity, heart disease and other health problems. However, fat is essential to the body. It insulates its systems from the cold and cushions its organs. Fat also helps process some vitamins and minerals and is one of the body's energy stores.

There are three main types of fat in our food, as shown in Table 5.1.

Key terms

Health – a state of physical and mental well-being where your body is free of disease and is working as it should.

Pulses – the edible seeds of certain plants. Lentils, peas and beans are pulses.

Did you know?

Fats are also called lipids.

Table 5.1: Types of fat.

Type of fat	Description
Saturated fat	• Considered the most harmful fat – too much can cause clogged arteries, leading to heart disease. • Normally solid at room temperature. • Found primarily in animal products (like meat, butter and lard) but also in some vegetable products (like coconut oil and palm oil).
Polyunsaturated fat	• Considered less damaging to the body than saturated fat. • Normally liquid at room temperature. • Found in a number of vegetable oils (like corn oil) and oily fish.
Monounsaturated fat	• Considered to be the healthiest of all three fats – may help to lower cholesterol levels. • Normally liquid at room temperature. • Found in foods such as olive oil, rapeseed oil, nuts and seeds.

The fats that you eat are broken down in the digestive system by an enzyme called lipase. This ensures that they are ready to be transported in the bloodstream. The fats are then either used as fuel or stored in fat deposits in our body.

Just checking

1 Which type of fat is considered the healthiest?
2 Where can you find saturated fat?
3 Which type of fat is liquid at room temperature?

Vitamins

Vitamins are essential nutrients that your body needs in small quantities to work properly. The human body needs a variety of different vitamins, including vitamins A, B, C and D. There are two types of vitamins: fat-soluble vitamins and water-soluble vitamins.

Fat-soluble vitamins are found in fatty foods such as animal fats (including butter and lard), vegetable oils, dairy foods, liver and oily fish. You do not need to eat these every day because your body stores these vitamins in your liver and fatty tissues for future use.

Fat-soluble vitamins are vitamin A, vitamin D, vitamin E and vitamin K.

Water-soluble vitamins are found in fruit, vegetables and grains. Water-soluble vitamins are not stored in the body, so you need to eat them more frequently. They can be destroyed by heat or by exposure to the air, and can be lost in cooking water.

Water-soluble vitamins are vitamin B, folic acid and vitamin C.

Table 5.2 shows the 13 different vitamins needed for good health.

Did you know?

There is not just one vitamin B – there is a whole family of B vitamins. This is known as the vitamin B complex.

Table 5.2: Vitamins required in a healthy diet.

Vitamin	Description
Vitamin A	• Important for healthy eyes, skin and immune system. • Found in foods including cheese, eggs and yoghurt, as well as in carrots, sweet potato and spinach.
Vitamin B complex	• **B1** – plays a vital part in converting the food you eat into energy; found in most types of food. • **B2** – important for healthy skin, eyes and nervous system; found in foods such as milk, eggs and rice. • **B3** – helps to produce energy from the food you eat and to keep the nervous and digestive systems healthy; found in foods including meat, fish, flour, eggs and milk. • **B5** – helps release energy from the food you eat; found in almost all meat and vegetable foods. • **B6** – allows the body to use and store energy from protein and carbohydrates; found in foods such as fish, whole cereals, eggs, vegetables and soya beans. • **B12** – used in the production of red blood cells and in the release of energy from the food you eat; found mostly in animal-based foods such as meat, fish, eggs and cheese.

continued

Table 5.2 continued

Vitamin	Description
Folic acid (Vitamin B9)	• Important for the nervous system, especially in unborn babies. • Found in foods including broccoli, spinach, liver, chickpeas and brown rice.
Vitamin C	• Helps the immune system fight off infection and viruses, and helps your body to repair itself after injury. • Found in fruit and vegetables, including citrus fruit (such as oranges and limes), strawberries, potatoes and broccoli.
Vitamin D	• Helps regulate the amount of calcium and phosphorus in the body, which are needed in the production of healthy bones. • Manufactured in the body from exposure to sunlight. • Also found in foods such as oily fish, eggs and fortified breakfast cereals.
Vitamin E	• Helps to protect the body from damage and boosts the immune system. • Found in plant oils such as olive oil and corn oil, nuts and seeds.
Vitamin K	• Essential in blood clotting, which is when your body forms scabs and repairs damaged blood vessels to stop bleeding. • Found in green leafy vegetables such as broccoli, vegetable oils and cereals.
Biotin	• Essential in the production of glycogen, which is the energy source for muscles. • Found in egg yolk, liver and yeast.

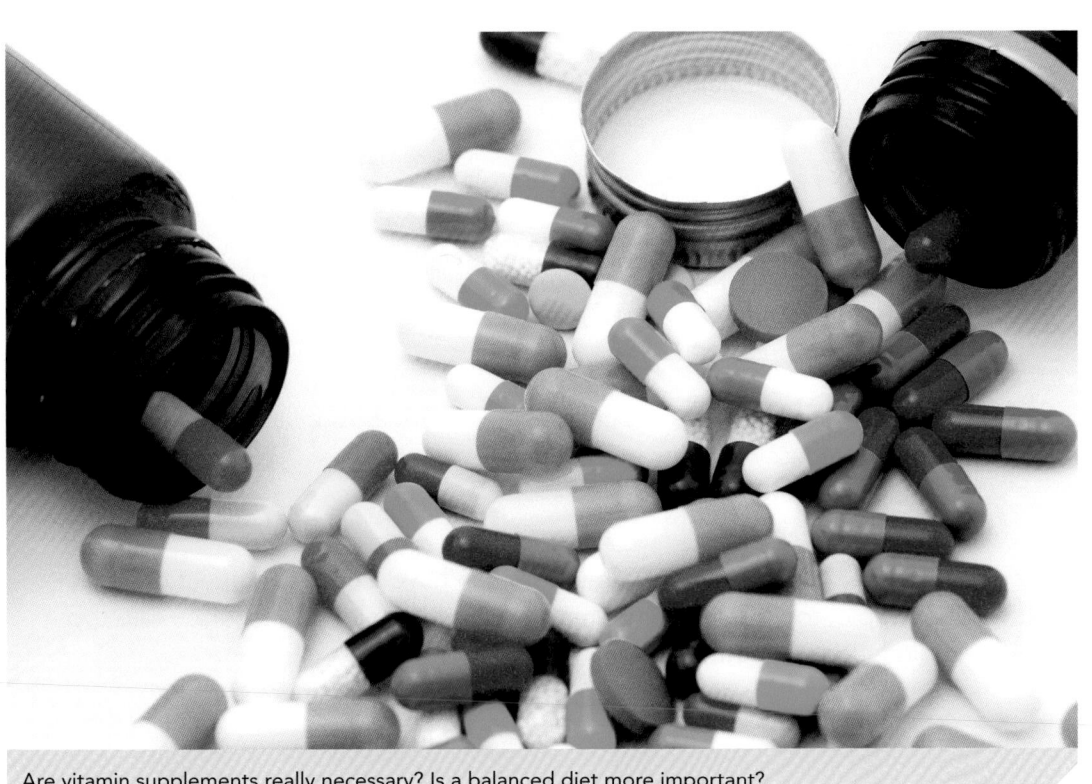

Are vitamin supplements really necessary? Is a balanced diet more important?

Minerals

Minerals are substances which the body needs in order to work properly.

We need more of some minerals than others. The minerals that we do not need much of are called 'trace minerals', because you only need a trace of them in your diet.

Key terms

Metabolism – the rate at which you use the energy in the food you eat. Nutrients that are processed into energy are 'metabolised'.

Anaemia – a lack of iron in the body, which makes you tired and pale.

Table 5.3: Common minerals, their functions and their sources.

Mineral	Main function	Good sources
Calcium	Builds strong bones and teeth.	Milk and other dairy produce, green vegetables, nuts and soya beans.
Iron	Helps make red blood cells.	Meat, brown rice and most dark green vegetables.
Iodine	Helps keep cells and **metabolism** healthy.	Sea fish and shellfish.
Magnesium	Helps turn food into energy and keeps bones healthy.	Green leafy vegetables, nuts, wholegrain bread and brown rice.
Manganese	Helps to make and activate enzymes in the body.	Tea, cereals, nuts, bread and green vegetables.
Phosphorus	Helps to build strong bones and teeth and to turn food into energy.	Dairy produce, bread, red meat, fish and poultry.
Potassium and sodium	Control balance of fluids in the body.	Potassium – vegetables, fruit such as bananas, fish, poultry and milk. Sodium – salt.
Selenium	Helps our immune system function and involved in reproduction.	Meat, fish and brazil nuts.
Zinc	Helps to make new cells, process nutrients in the food you eat and heal wounds.	Meat, shellfish, bread and dairy products.

Having too much or too little of some minerals can have a negative effect on your health. For example, too much sodium may lead to high blood pressure, while too little iron could lead to **anaemia**.

Water

Water makes up about two-thirds of the human body. This constantly needs to be replaced as we lose water through respiration, sweating and urination. An average adult can lose around 2.5 litres of water a day, so a person doing a strenuous job or exercise will lose a lot more than that.

No system in the body could survive without water. Many people do not drink enough water to replace the losses that occur naturally in the body, and this can lead to headaches, tiredness and dizziness.

Fibre

Fibre is part of plants. Most of it is not digested, but it is used to push food through our digestive system. Good sources of fibre include oats, beans, unpeeled potatoes and wholegrain foods such as brown pasta or wholemeal bread. Eating enough fibre may also protect you from bowel cancer.

Just checking

1 How many vitamins does our body need?

2 What percentage of the human body is water?

3 What are minerals?

▶ Food groups and a balanced diet

Your diet is all of the food you eat. A balanced diet includes food from all the five main food groups, which are:

- fruit and vegetables
- bread, rice, cereals and pasta
- milk and dairy products
- meat, fish and alternatives
- food containing fat and sugar.

Fruit and vegetables

Current government advice is to eat at least five portions of fruit and vegetables each day. These portions can be fresh, tinned, frozen or juiced. Examples of a 'portion' include:

- a banana, apple or orange
- one glass of fruit juice
- three heaped tablespoons of cooked vegetables like peas or carrots.

Fruit and vegetables are a good source of the vitamins and minerals which the body needs. They are also a good source of fibre, which helps keep the digestive system healthy.

Bread, rice, cereals, pasta

This food group includes bread, breakfast cereals, oats, pasta, rice, noodles and potatoes. These foods provide complex carbohydrates which can leave you feeling full for longer, as well as vitamins and minerals such as iron and B vitamins. This group is an important source of energy for the body.

Take it further

Keep a diary for a week in which you record the amount of fruit and vegetables you eat during that week. How many portions do you eat per day? What could you do to increase your intake of fruit and vegetables?

Milk and dairy products

This food group includes foods such as cheese, milk and yoghurt. Dairy foods are rich in calcium, vitamin B12 and protein, and they are important in making strong teeth and bones.

Meat, fish and alternatives

This food group contains meat, meat products such as sausages and beef burgers, fish, and fish products such as fish fingers and fishcakes. It also includes eggs and offal such as liver and kidneys. Not everything in this group is actually meat or fish: it also includes vegetarian alternatives such as chickpeas, lentils and nuts. They are all good sources of protein, which is used for the growth and repair of muscles, skin and other parts of the body.

Food high in fat and sugar

The group of foods containing fat and sugar includes butter, cream, chocolate, fizzy drinks, ice creams, biscuits, mayonnaise, cakes and pastries, sweet puddings and desserts. They often provide the body with far more energy than it needs and this can lead to the surplus being stored as fat.

Diets in the western world tend to contain too much fat, sugar and salt, which can cause problems such as obesity, high blood pressure, coronary heart disease and dental decay.

The eatwell plate

The eatwell plate in Figure 5.2 shows a balanced healthy diet. This consists of enough of each of the food groups to satisfy the needs of the body without having too much of any one food group.

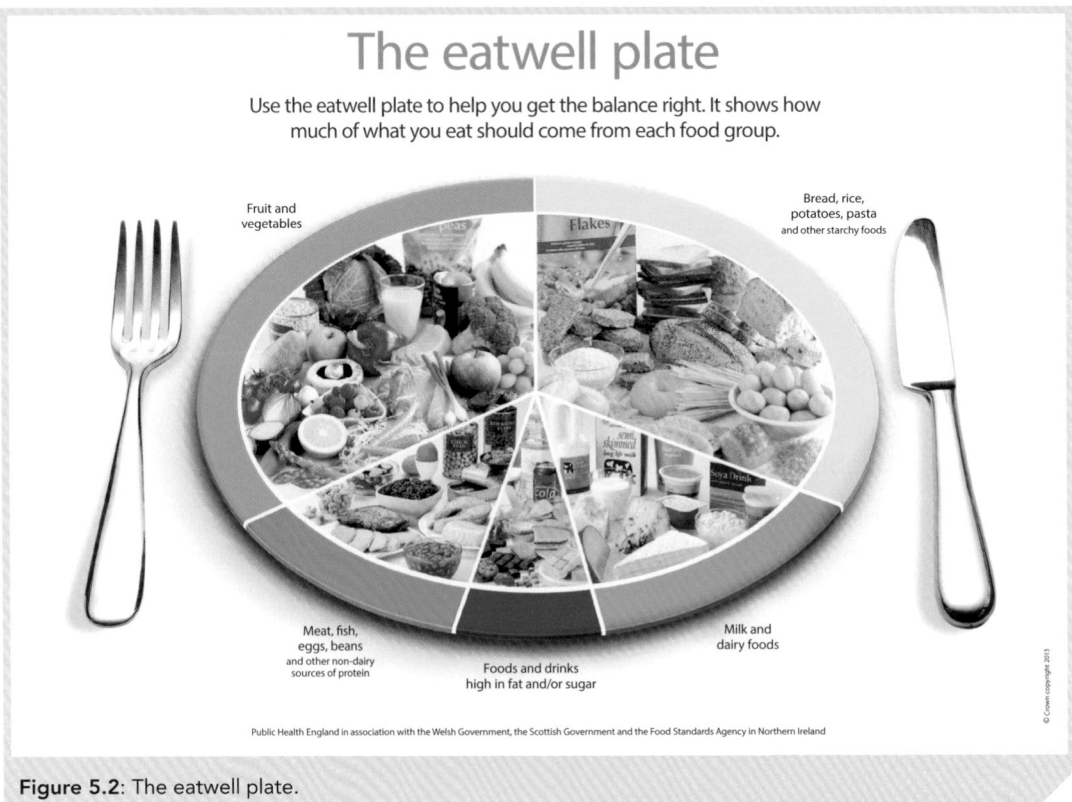

Figure 5.2: The eatwell plate.

Recommended daily allowances (RDAs)

An RDA of a nutrient is the amount that the government and health authorities suggest you should eat or drink in order to maintain good health. This is shown in Table 5.4.

Table 5.4: Recommended daily allowances in the UK.

	Women	Men
Calories (kcals)	2000	2500
Total fat	70 g	95 g
Saturated fat	20 g	30 g
Carbohydrates	230 g	300 g
Sugars	50 g	70 g
Protein	45 g	55 g
Salt	6 g max	6 g max
Water and drinks	1.6 litres	2 litres
Alcohol	2–3 units maximum	3–4 units maximum

Remember

A unit of alcohol is 10 ml of pure alcohol. It takes an average adult about an hour to process this until there is none left in the bloodstream.

- A small glass of wine contains 1.5 units.
- A pint of lager contains 2–3 units.
- A single small shot of spirits contains 1 unit.

Some food packaging includes a colour-coded 'traffic light' label, like that shown in Figure 5.3. This label shows how much of each nutrient a single serving of the food contains and displays it as a percentage of your RDA.

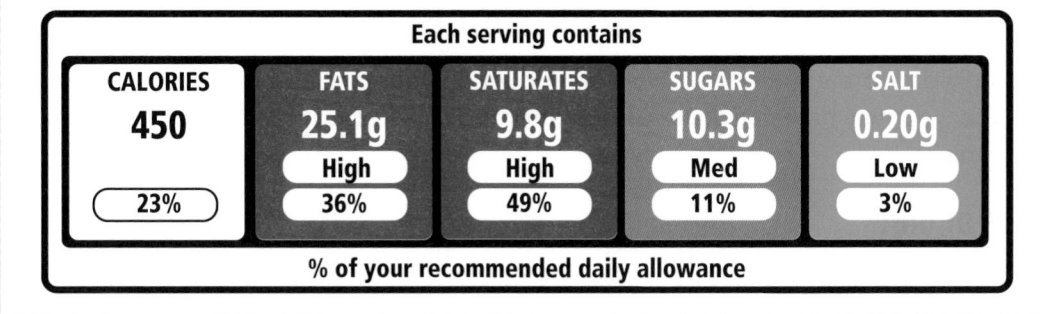

Each serving contains				
CALORIES	**FATS**	**SATURATES**	**SUGARS**	**SALT**
450	**25.1g**	**9.8g**	**10.3g**	**0.20g**
	High	High	Med	Low
23%	36%	49%	11%	3%
	% of your recommended daily allowance			

Figure 5.3: A food label showing RDAs.

Take it further

Keep the food labels for everything you eat on a particular day. At the end of the day add up all the amounts to see if you have eaten more or less than your RDAs. How did you do?

Remember that dietary requirements vary from person to person. They depend on your current weight, level of physical activity and current health. The figures in Table 5.4 are guideline amounts.

Activity 5.1 | The eatwell plate

The eatwell plate shows the proportions of each type of food that should make up a healthy diet.

1 What are the five food groups?
2 Name three foods that belong in each group.
3 What are the most important nutrients in each group? Why are they important for health?

Diet and the home environment

Diet can also be affected by environmental factors. These are things in your surroundings which affect your behaviour, and include money and time.

Money

Nutritious food can be more expensive than foods that are high in fat and sugar. Many households struggle to buy enough nutritious food and rely instead on cheaper alternatives. It is estimated that, in 2012, 13 million people in the UK were living in poverty. These people are not just those who have to claim state benefits, but also millions of people who are paid very low wages.

Time

In working families, it can be difficult to find the time to cook and prepare healthy meals from scratch. Reheatable ready meals are popular because they are convenient, but these meals are often high in salt, fat and sugar.

Discussion

Do you know how to cook basic dishes? When did you last cook for your family? Consider your cooking skills and how you could learn to cook cheap nutritious food.

Diet and individual preferences

Your individual preferences also have an impact on your diet and food choices. For example, you may have food allergies or strong dislikes about food which influence your choices.

Types of diet

You may have a different diet because of religious or ethical beliefs. Some of these types of diet are shown in Table 5.5.

Table 5.5: Some different types of diet.

Type of diet	Description
Halal	• A halal diet abides by the principles of Islam. • Permitted foods are called halal. Forbidden foods are called haram. • A halal diet will not include alcohol, pork or pork products. • Animals used for meat must be killed in a certain way.

continued

Table 5.5 continued

Type of diet	Description
Kosher	• A kosher diet abides by the principles of Judaism. • A kosher diet will not include pork and pork products. Meat and dairy food should also not be eaten together. • Animals used for meat must be killed in a certain way.
Vegan	• A vegan will not eat any food from animals at all. They rely completely on a plant-based diet. • Vegans must ensure that their diet contains enough protein, calcium, iron and vitamin B12, which is difficult because most sources of these are animal-based.
Vegetarian	• A vegetarian will not eat meat or meat products. • Most vegetarians will eat products from animals, such as yoghurt, eggs and milk.

Choosing a balanced diet

A diet should not just be a way to lose weight – it is a **lifestyle** choice. Many people who have worked hard to lose weight find they put it back on again when they come off their restricted diet and begin to eat normally again. Instead, you should maintain a balanced diet throughout your life.

Eating for an active lifestyle

People with active jobs find that they are hungrier and eat more food than people who have desk jobs. This is because their bodies are using more energy. It is important to eat properly if you have a physically demanding job. For example, ration packs supplied to the armed forces contain up to 4000 kcal per 24 hours, rather than the recommended daily allowance of 2000–2500 kcal.

Family history

A family history of particular medical conditions, such as high blood pressure or diabetes, can be one of the first indicators of your own personal health risks. You may be able to reduce the risks of developing similar conditions through better diet and **nutrition**.

Key terms

Lifestyle – this is the way you choose to live your life. Lifestyle choices include factors such as your leisure activities, dress, diet and your personal relationships.

Nutrition – the study of how the body uses foods and nutrients vital to health in the growth, maintenance and reproduction of cells.

Activity 5.2	Your personal health risks

Ask yourself the following questions.

1 Does your family have a history of any medical conditions that might affect your health in the future?

2 Are any of these medical conditions a problem if you want to join a public service?

3 Can you prevent or control any of these medical conditions through a better diet or better nutrition?

The impact of nutrition on personal health

Nutrition can have a huge impact on personal health. There is a range of conditions which can be affected by your diet, and these should be tested for and monitored.

Hypoglycaemia

Hypoglycaemia is very low blood sugar, so the body does not have enough energy to carry out all of its activities. This can lead to sweating, feeling hungry, confusion and poor concentration. In severe cases, people can lose consciousness. If you become hypoglycaemic, you should have some food or drink that contains sugar.

Diabetes

Diabetes is a condition where the body has trouble making or using the hormone insulin. Insulin is important because it helps turn sugar and other food into energy. A lack of insulin can cause blood sugar levels to become too high. Having high blood sugar levels over long periods of time can be dangerous – it can cause problems with the eyes and vision, as well as increasing the risk of heart attacks and strokes.

There are two types of diabetes:

- type 1 – the body does not produce insulin. Type 1 diabetes cannot be prevented, as the body's own immune system destroys the cells that make insulin
- type 2 – the body does not produce enough insulin, or the cells cannot use insulin properly. Some instances of type 2 diabetes can be prevented by healthy diet and exercise.

Activity 5.3   Diabetes warning signs

Some common early warning signs of diabetes include:

- always being thirsty
- always being tired
- needing to urinate a lot
- losing weight quickly.

Produce a poster which could be used in your school or college which tells people the warning signs and where they should go for help if they recognise any of the signs of diabetes.

Obesity

Obesity is when a person is so overweight that their weight is seriously endangering their health. It is on the increase due to the availability of high fat and sugar foods and snacks, and a decrease in the amount of exercise we take. Obesity increases the risk of heart disease and strokes and is a key issue for the public services.

Did you know?

High blood sugar is called hyperglycaemia and low blood sugar is called hypoglycaemia. This is because 'hyper' means 'over' and 'hypo' means 'under'.

Take it further

Insulin is the hormone produced by the pancreas that allows sugar to enter the body's cells, where it is used as fuel for energy. Carry out some research on insulin and identify the risk factors for diabetes.

Did you know?

In 2012, 26% of all adults and 14% of children aged 2–10 years were obese. Diseases caused by poor diet and sedentary lifestyles cost the NHS more than £6 billion each year.

Blood pressure

Blood pressure is the force that your heart exerts to move blood around your body. High blood pressure can be very serious but rarely has any obvious symptoms. It is thought that around 30% of adults in England have high blood pressure, but that many are unaware of it. If left untreated, it can cause heart attacks and strokes.

Cholesterol

Cholesterol is a type of fat produced by the liver, but you can also get it by eating certain foods. It is essential for good health because it helps your brain, skin and other organs to grow and do their jobs. However, having too much of it can cause problems.

If you have too much cholesterol in your blood, it can collect on the walls of the blood vessels in your body, causing them to become narrower. This can clog the blood vessels and stop the blood moving freely throughout your body. Over many years, if the clogging gets worse, it can completely block a blood vessel, which leads to a heart attack or stroke.

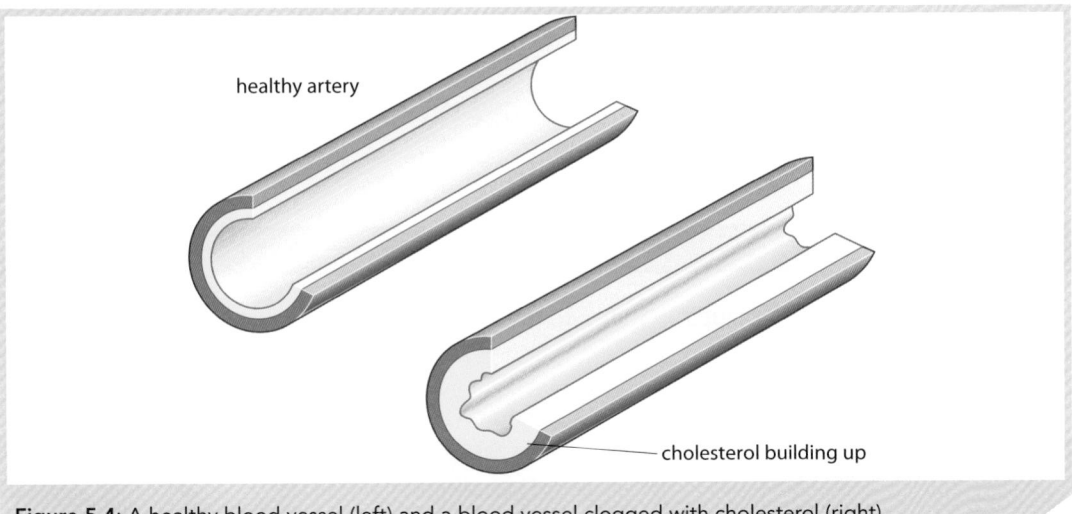

healthy artery

cholesterol building up

Figure 5.4: A healthy blood vessel (left) and a blood vessel clogged with cholesterol (right).

Activity 5.4 Cholesterol

1 Why is cholesterol good for your body?
2 What can happen if you have high cholesterol levels over a long period?
3 What can you do to reduce your cholesterol levels?
4 How can you find out if your cholesterol levels are too high?

Heart disease

Heart disease occurs when the arteries and blood vessels that supply the heart with oxygen become narrowed and blocked by a gradual build up of fatty material. The lack of oxygen to the heart can cause pain and discomfort. This condition is called angina.

If part of the fatty material breaks off it can block a blood vessel, which deprives a part of the heart of its oxygen supply. This is known as a heart attack, and can cause permanent damage and even death.

 Take it further

Do some independent research and identify which factors can increase the risk of heart disease. Do you have any of these risk factors? What could you do to ensure your heart remains healthy?

Effects of poor diet and nutrition

A poor diet can have several effects on your health and fitness. Some of these are shown in Table 5.6.

Key terms

Lethargy – feeling sluggish and lacking in energy.

Fitness – your ability to perform a particular task or set of tasks. The level of fitness required for particular tasks will vary.

Table 5.6: Effects of poor diet and nutrition.

Effect	Description
Lethargy	Lack of food can make you feel lethargic. It can be difficult to motivate yourself when you feel this way.
Obesity	Obesity is usually caused by eating too much food with high fat and sugar content and by a lack of exercise. It can have serious health consequences.
Susceptibility to injury or illness	Poor diet can leave you vulnerable to being injured or becoming ill, e.g. if your diet does not contain enough vitamins and minerals you risk getting illnesses.
Lack of concentration	Poor diet or lack of food can affect concentration. This can have serious consequences in the public services, where the ability to focus and concentrate is a key skill.

Just checking

1 What are the five food groups included on the eatwell plate?
2 What is hypoglycaemia?

▶ Lifestyle factors that affect health and fitness

Introduction

Your lifestyle can have a significant effect on your health. The way you live your life and the choices you make can lead to good health and fitness or poor health and fitness. It is important to understand how the things you choose to do and eat can affect your body. How do you feel after a sleepless night? Do you struggle at school the next day?

An active lifestyle which includes regular exercise or planned participation in sport, a balanced diet and enough sleep will have a positive impact on an individual's health and fitness.

Benefits of exercise

Individuals who exercise regularly, either as part of their job or in their leisure time, have fewer heart attacks than those who do not. Exercise builds up the strength of the heart, which means it can cope better if you put a sudden physical demand on it. Exercise can also:

- help reduce your risk of heart disease, stroke and type 2 diabetes
- help you maintain a healthy weight
- lower your risk of bone deterioration as you age
- keep your muscles strong and joints flexible
- help you cope with stress and depression
- promote psychological well-being and positive self-image
- give you an opportunity to meet and socialise with other people, perhaps in the gym or as part of a sports team.

A healthy diet

See Topic A.1 (pages 134–146) for more information about the importance of a healthy diet.

Sleep

Sleep is a regular period of unconsciousness. It is unclear why we need sleep, but it is thought that sleep recharges the brain.

A lack of sleep can severely affect mental and physical performance, and can cause irritability, headaches, memory lapses and delayed reactions.

It is thought that the health of people with disturbed sleep patterns, such as shift workers, may suffer as a result of this. This has particular consequences for the public services, which often operate rotating shift patterns.

Why is it so important to get enough sleep?

Good personal hygiene

Keeping clean is an essential part of any lifestyle. Regular washing removes sweat and dirt, preventing unpleasant smells and reducing the risk of infection. This is especially important for personnel in the armed services operating away from their base for an extended period of time, for example in jungle conditions where bacteria can thrive.

Emergency services personnel may come into contact with contaminated environments such as tanker spillages or crime scenes involving blood and other bodily fluids. These environments can pose a significant threat to health and safety if you neglect your personal hygiene.

There are several easy ways of promoting good personal hygiene, including:

- daily washing, especially after physical activity
- washing your hands before eating
- washing food before eating it if you suspect it may be dirty
- wearing clean clothes every day if possible
- wearing protective equipment you are given, such as gloves or eye shields.

Case study

Jack is a 23-year-old who wants to apply for a career in the Royal Marines. His lifestyle over the last couple of years has not been good for his health and fitness. Jack's lifestyle factors include:

- frequently eating takeaway food
- occasionally taking illegal drugs
- drinking alcohol to excess at least three times per week
- smoking heavily
- doing little physical activity.

Jack is aware that his lifestyle has to change and he needs to clean up his act before he can apply to the service of his choice.

1 What should Jack's first lifestyle change be?

2 Where could Jack get help to improve his lifestyle?

3 What will be the consequences if Jack does not change his lifestyle, both long-term and short-term?

4 What impact will Jack's current lifestyle have had on his health and fitness?

5 Design a lifestyle action plan to help Jack improve his chances of succeeding on the Potential Royal Marines' Course.

Key terms

Respiratory – associated with the intake and expiration of oxygen. The respiratory system includes your nose, mouth, larynx and lungs.

Endorphins – hormones released in the brain and nervous sytem.

▶ Occasional exercise

Occasional exercise can have a number of good effects on the body. However, if the body is not accustomed to exercise, occasional exercise can lead to injury. Table 5.7 shows some of the main effects of occasional exercise on the body.

Table 5.7: Positive and negative effects of occasional exercise.

Positive effects	Description
Increased metabolism	There is some evidence to suggest that exercising boosts the metabolism to burn more calories and fat.
Improved muscle tone	Exercise develops muscle tone, which helps support good posture and makes daily tasks easier. This can help to prevent injury by reducing the strain on muscles, tendons and ligaments.
Improved respiratory capacity	Improved **respiratory** capacity allows the body to perform exercise much more efficiently. This is because the respiratory system is more effective in getting oxygen into the bloodstream, transporting it to the working muscles and getting rid of carbon dioxide.
Release of **endorphins**	Endorphins are produced in response to stress or pain. They work mainly in parts of the brain responsible for pleasure and blocking pain.

Negative effect	Description
Strains and pulled muscles	It can be easy to pull a muscle or strain tendons and ligaments if your body is not used to exercise or if you do not know how to exercise correctly. This can be very painful and may take days or weeks to recover.

Smoking, drinking and the use of drugs

Smoking, drinking and the use of drugs can have a significant impact on individuals' health and fitness. Use of these substances can range from casual recreational use to addiction. When misused, these substances can have a negative impact on physical and mental health, and personal hygiene.

The impact of smoking

Smoking is a major health risk. It can cause heart disease, numerous cancers and bronchial disorders. Over 100,000 people die every year from smoking-related diseases. According to the NHS, smoking increases a person's risk of developing heart disease by 24%.

The body becomes addicted to the nicotine in tobacco. Nicotine is a **stimulant**, which means that it makes the heart beat faster and narrows the blood vessels. This causes a strain on the cardiovascular system. The carbon monoxide in cigarette smoke also reduces the capacity of the blood to carry oxygen to the tissues, which means that the heart must work even harder.

Smoking decreases your lung capacity, which can have a serious effect on your fitness. It damages the alveoli in your lungs, which are small air sacs that absorb oxygen as you inhale and pass it through the blood to your organs. If the alveoli become too damaged you will struggle to get the oxygen you need in order to do physical activity. In the short term, it can also increase existing problems such as asthma, which might compromise your performance.

Smoking leaves a distinctive smell on your hair, skin and clothes, which is not the image the public services want to promote. Dealing with addiction can also have an impact on your mental health, particularly if you want to give up smoking and cannot.

The impact of alcohol

Alcohol has an impact on all of the major body systems and alcohol abuse can lead to death. Some of the possible effects of drinking more alcohol than the recommended levels are liver cancer, liver disease, cancer of the mouth, neck and throat and high blood pressure. Alcohol also impairs your decision making and increases your risk of accidents.

In public service work, the use of alcohol can directly affect your work. Many public service jobs require the operation of equipment such as breathing apparatus, weapons or vehicles. However, the presence of alcohol in your system will impair your judgement, placing yourself and others at risk.

In addition, alcohol is very high in calories and can lead to weight gain. Carrying excess weight places an additional strain on systems such as the **cardiovascular** and respiratory systems. Like cigarette smoke, the smell of alcohol is distinctive and can stay on your breath for some time.

 Key terms

Stimulant – a substance that raises the body's level of physiological or nervous activity.

Cardiovascular – associated with blood flow and circulation. The cardiovascular system includes your heart and blood vessels.

 Did you know?

Smoking is thought to cost the NHS £5 billion per year.

 Remember

It is very important that you never drink while you are working. To do so is likely to lead to a formal disciplinary hearing and even dismissal from the public services.

The impact of drugs

The abuse of illegal drugs can have a variety of effects on the short- and long-term health and fitness of an individual. Some common drugs and some of their side effects are:

- **opiates** (such as heroin) – side effects include addiction, nausea and vomiting, vein damage from injection, fatal respiratory failure, HIV and hepatitis spread by sharing contaminated needles
- **amphetamines** (also known as speed or whizz) – side effects include agitation and panic attacks, psychosis, heart strain, over-activity and sleeplessness, a lowered immune system
- **LSD** (also known as acid) – side effects include sensory distortions, hallucinations, feelings of panic or anxiety
- **ecstasy** (also known as E) – side effects include overheating, dehydration, panic attacks, paranoia
- **cocaine** – side effects include heart failure, damage to nasal septum, paranoia, breathing problems, vein damage from injecting.

Drug misuse may lead to unwise sexual behaviour or involvement in crime.

In sports, people may also use performance-enhancing drugs such as anabolic steroids. They are taken by some athletes and bodybuilders to increase their muscle mass and strength, but can also have serious side effects such as:

- in men – shrunken testicles, baldness, a higher voice, prominent breasts and infertility
- in women – a deeper voice, baldness, and increased facial and body hair.

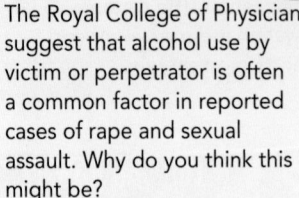

Discussion

The Royal College of Physicians suggest that alcohol use by victim or perpetrator is often a common factor in reported cases of rape and sexual assault. Why do you think this might be?

▶ Sexual health

Your sexual health and behaviour can have a significant impact on many areas of your life, including your sleep patterns, your risk of sexually transmitted disease and your emotional well-being.

Sleep patterns

Not getting enough sleep can cause significant short- and long-term problems, including:

- feeling tired
- irritability
- lack of concentration
- sleeping at inappropriate moments, such as while driving
- depressed immune system, which leaves you vulnerable to disease and infection
- slowed reaction times.

Activity 5.5   Consequences of bad sleep

Consider the problems which can be caused by a lack of sleep listed above. How would these affect the performance of a police officer? What might be the consequences for the public and for the officer's colleagues? Discuss your thoughts and list your answers.

Sexually transmitted infections (STIs)

Unprotected sexual activity can lead to the transmission of sexually transmitted infections such as herpes, genital warts, venereal disease and HIV. Although many STIs are easily treatable with antibiotics, some can do severe damage before symptoms begin to show. For example, pelvic inflammatory disease in women can lead to permanent infertility. Some STIs cannot be cured, including herpes and HIV.

There is also a link between unprotected sexual intercourse and a virus called human papilloma virus (HPV), which is thought to cause cervical and anal cancer.

To combat some of these problems the use of a condom is crucial and can protect against many (though not all) STIs. In addition, the NHS recommends that women should have regular cervical smears after the age of 25.

Because your sexual lifestyle can have long-term implications for your health, it is important to be responsible. The excessive use of alcohol can lead to unwise and unsafe sexual behaviour, which increases the risk of sexual assault, unplanned pregnancy and STIs.

Emotional impact

If your sexual health is compromised, this can have a significant emotional impact on you. Sexually transmitted infections can cause people a great deal of embarrassment and shame, and this can make them unnecessarily worried about seeking treatment. It can also have an impact on your personal relationships.

Assessment activity 5.1

Your local residential home for older people is holding a promotional event to help elderly people become physically active. They have asked you to help them design a booklet and presentation which could be used at the event. The presentation will be shown throughout the day on television screens and the booklet will be given to everyone who attends. There will also be demonstrations of physical activity that will suit all ages and ability, such as ballroom dancing, bowling and pilates.

Remember to consider the effect that the elderly residents' nutrition has on their health and fitness. You should talk about the effects of their lifestyle on their health and fitness. Your presentation and booklet also need to provide some guidance on how people attending the day might improve their health and fitness.

What impact might poor sexual health have on your relationships?

Tip

- Consider the key elements of nutrition and lifestyle on a person's overall health and use your booklet and presentation to help them think about how they could improve their lifestyle.

▶ Public service job requirements for health and/or fitness

Introduction

Most of the uniformed public services have some kind of fitness assessment that you must pass in order to be considered for employment. Fitness is really important to the public services as the nature of their work is very physically active. How active are you? Do you exercise regularly? If not, why not?

Link

See Unit 1 (pages 4–16) for more information on public service groups.

The public service sector can be divided into different types of public service groups, including:

- emergency services (Police, Fire and Rescue, and Ambulance Services)
- armed services (British Army, Royal Navy, Royal Air Force)
- local authorities
- central government
- voluntary services (for example British Red Cross, Samaritans, St John Ambulance).

Each of these groups has different requirements for health and fitness.

▶ Health and fitness requirements

There are specific roles within individual public services that require health and/or fitness entry requirements to determine an individual's suitability for that job.

Emergency services

The emergency services have highly specialised roles which require specific skills and levels of fitness. These requirements are necessary to ensure that an individual, such as a police officer or firefighter, is fit enough to do their job properly.

For example, in order to join the Fire and Rescue Service, potential firefighters must pass six nationally-set tests. These test applicants' fitness, strength and dexterity, which are all key skills in fighting fires. The tasks also test confidence under pressure, which is another key attribute a firefighter needs in order to do their job.

These tests include:

- a ladder climb – wearing full rescue equipment, candidates climb a fully extended 13.5 m ladder and demonstrate a 'leg lock'
- a casualty evacuation – a 55 kg dummy casualty is dragged around a 30 m course safely and at walking speed
- an enclosed space test – wearing full rescue equipment, candidates negotiate their way through crawl spaces and walkways.

Why do you think firefighters need to be physically fit?

Activity 5.6   Fitness for the Police Service

Research the fitness tests which applicants to the Police Service must pass. Produce a booklet which clearly explains each test and the standards you need to achieve in order to pass.

Case study

Individuals who want to be prison officers take a fitness assessment during an HM Prison Service assessment day. The fitness tests include:

- grip strength test – this involves holding a dynamometer in both hands and squeezing it as hard as possible
- multi-stage fitness test – this is a shuttle run over a 15 m course
- dynamic strength test – this involves completing a set of upper body pulls and pushes to assess strength
- speed agility run test – this involves moving as quickly as you can while negotiating obstacles and changing direction
- shield test – this involves holding a static position while holding a 6 kg shield during control and restraint techniques.

1 Why do you think prison officers need to be physically fit?

2 In what circumstances would a prison officer need to use the physical skills described above?

3 Conduct some research – what are the non-physical tests a potential prison officer has to pass in addition to the fitness tests described above?

Armed services

The armed services require a high standard of physical fitness due to the strenuous nature of their operational work.

Did you know? ?

The PJFT consists of two 2.4 km runs conducted on a running machine with a 2% incline. The first 2.4 km run needs to be completed in under 12 minutes and 30 seconds. The second run must be completed in under 10 minutes.

One of the toughest physical fitness tests of any armed service is conducted by the Royal Marines. This is called the Potential Royal Marines Course (PRMC) and requires very high standards of physical fitness. Before taking the actual test, candidates must pass a pre-joining fitness test (PJFT) to test their fitness before they can proceed to the PRMC.

The PRMC is a non-stop two-day challenge, including assault courses, fitness tests, shooting, interviews and drill (see Table 5.8). Like the Royal Navy, the Royal Marines are experts in waterborne combat and so swimming tests are an essential component of the course.

Table 5.8: The schedule of the Potential Royal Marines Course (PRMC).

Day	Component	Description
Day 1	Computer-based tests	A series of English and maths tests.
	3 mile run	1.5 miles as a squad in under 12 minutes 30 seconds and 1.5 miles individually in under 10 minutes 30 seconds.
	Gym test 1	• Bleep test (reach level 13 for maximum points). • Press-ups (60 within 2 minutes for maximum points). • Sit-ups (80 in 2 minutes for maximum points). • Pull-ups (target of 8 quality pull-ups).
	Interview	A formal interview with the PRMC officer.
Day 2	Confidence test and assault course	This test is carried out regardless of the weather. It takes over 2 hours to complete.
	High obstacle course	This test involves climbing ladders, moving across ropes and negotiating other obstacles up to 30 feet off the ground. It also includes a timed run around the course.
	Endurance course	This lasts 90 minutes and covers more than 2.5 miles of cross-country ground, including tunnels and water obstacles.
	Overnight	This involves spending the night out in the open. Candidates will work with others to prepare shelter and food.
Day 3	3.5 mile run	Candidates run back to camp.

Take it further

Research the physical fitness requirements for other public service jobs such as a pilot or a soldier, or for the particular service you are interested in.

At all times, recruits are observed to see if they have the qualities required to be a Royal Marine Commando. The PRMC is one of the most physically demanding selection courses, but is good preparation for the 32-week Commando training course.

Local authorities and central government

It would be very unusual for a local authority or central government to require a physical fitness test for entry to any of its jobs. Although some local authority roles require a good standard of health and fitness, such as a refuse collector, there are no specific tests that need to be undertaken in order to be offered the job.

However, working in central or local government can be very stressful and good health will help you deal with the pressures brought by working with the public every day. In jobs such as social work, there are no physical fitness requirements but the stress of the work requires a good standard of health.

Voluntary services

Since people give up their time for free to work for voluntary services, it can be very difficult for voluntary services to make their entry requirements too restrictive, as not many people would be prepared to undergo them. For example, St John Ambulance, who provide first aid support at events, only require volunteers to be 'fit for role' (that is, physically able to demonstrate basic life support).

Discussion

Why do you think the armed and emergency services have much more rigorous fitness testing than local government or voluntary services? Discuss the reasons and make a list of the top three.

Different requirements of the services

The fitness tests and health requirements you are asked for will differ between the services. This is because there are differences in the physical nature of the work undertaken by employees in each service.

For example, a firefighter needs different levels of fitness to a benefits officer, even though they both work in the public services. The fitness tests (if there are any) are designed to make sure you will be fit enough to do the job.

Some roles have ongoing fitness requirements. Reasons for ongoing fitness requirements are shown in Figure 5.5.

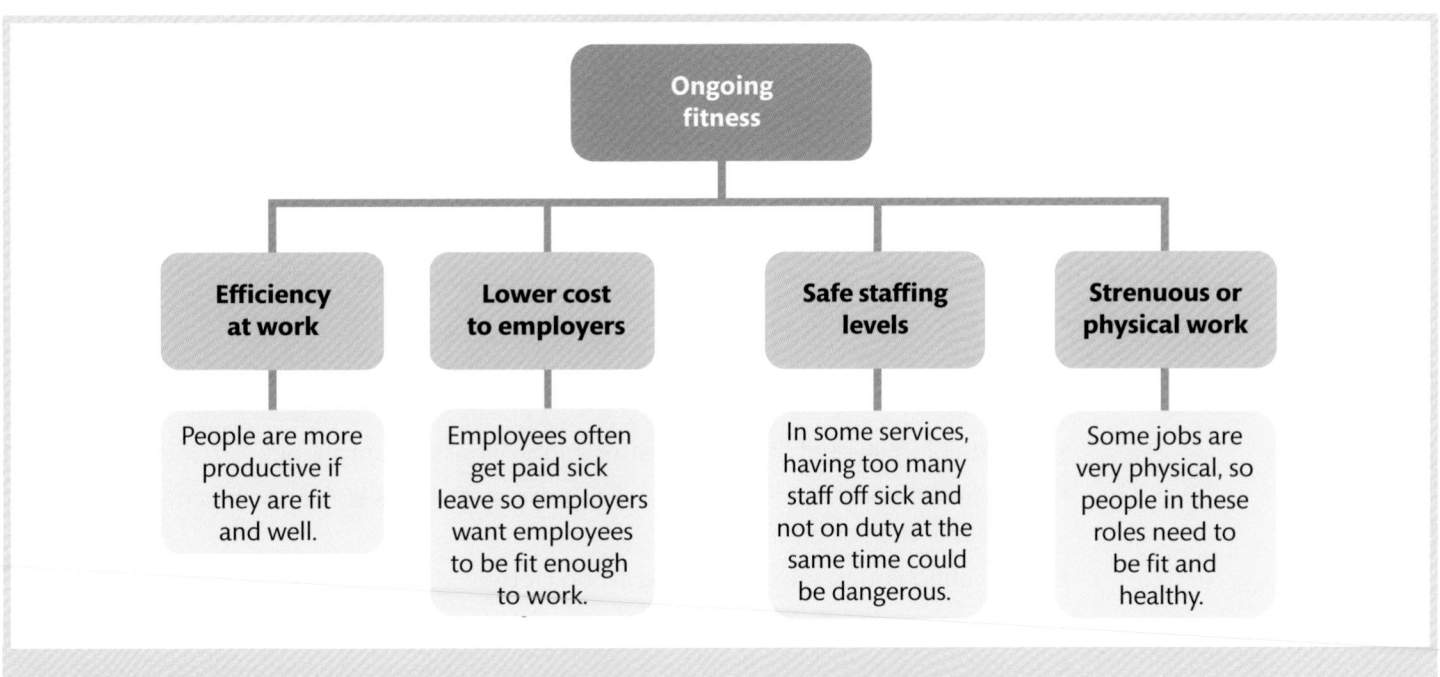

Figure 5.5: Reasons for fitness requirements in the public services.

Assessment activity 5.2

Your college has been contacted by a local secondary school asking if a group of public service students would be willing to plan and deliver a public service-style fitness day, including classroom-based sessions and practical activities. This is specifically for learners who are considering the public services as a career and who may join your course next year.

As part of the day you need to include:

- the health and fitness requirements for jobs within three different services
- why the services have fitness requirements in the first place
- the reasons why each service uses those particular tests
- the service you are interested in and the fitness tests for your chosen job.

Produce a set of slides and notes which cover the points above.

Tips

- Consider the range of public services you could cover. Choose from different groups – do not just choose three armed or three emergency services.
- Remember your audience – what do they need to know about the fitness requirements for working in the sector? Try to provide as much useful detail as you can.

 # Fitness tests

Introduction

The services use a wide range of tests in their selection process and it is important that you have the chance to practise some of them. Have you ever done any fitness tests before? What do you think are your strengths and what do you need to improve?

A wide range of tests are used by various public services to establish a candidate's fitness for entry or ongoing fitness. Other key reasons for undertaking a fitness test before you join a service include:

- assessing current levels of fitness
- providing an initial fitness level against which future progress can be monitored and measured
- ascertaining level of fitness loss after injury, illness or pregnancy
- allowing medical practitioners to recognise and assess some specific health problems such as heart disease
- motivating you to improve fitness to do better
- allowing you to see if a particular fitness programme is working
- making sure you are as fit to do a job now as you were when you joined a service. This is why some services have an annual fitness test.

Public service fitness tests and their protocols

The methods the public services use to test fitness and performance can differ from service to service. However, their purpose is always the same – to see if you are physically fit enough to take on the role you are applying for.

Generally speaking, public service performance assessments or fitness tests aim to determine your stamina and strength. Some of the tests that you might encounter in the public services are outlined below with a description of the protocol of each test.

Testing flexibility

- **The sit and reach test** – assesses flexibility. The individual sits down with their legs straight out in front of them and the soles of their feet flat against a box, which has a measuring device such as a ruler on top of it. They then reach forward with their fingertips to see how far past their toes they can reach. The movement should be smooth and continuous rather than lunging. The test is very easy to administer but it only assesses the flexibility of the hamstrings and lower back rather than of the whole body. Results are usually measured in centimetres.

Testing strength

- **The grip test** – measures the strength of an individual's grip using a grip strength dynamometer. The dynamometer is set at 0 and the handle adjusted to fit the size of the palm. Then the dynamometer is squeezed as hard as possible. The reading on the gauge tells you how strong your grip is. Most people find the hand that they use frequently is usually the stronger hand.
- **One repetition maximum (1RM) tests** – assess muscular strength. These tests measure the maximum weight that an individual can lift. They are normally done with free weights or standard gym equipment.

Testing aerobic endurance

- **The step test** – measures aerobic endurance. You step up and down from a step, usually around 12 inches high, for 3 minutes (or other set duration), then measure your heart rate. The lower your heart rate, the fitter you are.
- **The multi-stage fitness test (MSFT)** – involves continuous running between two markers set 20 m apart, in time with a set of pre-recorded bleeps. This is why the MSFT is often called the bleep test. The advantage of this test is that large numbers of people can be tested at the same time, but the disadvantage is that you need to be highly motivated to run until you cannot go any further.

Testing speed

- **60 m sprint** – assesses straight-line speed. A 60 m course is laid out and runners complete it as fast as possible. The results are recorded.

What physical abilities does the MSFT assess?

Testing power

Vertical and horizontal jumps – designed to measure explosive power in the legs.

- **The Sergent jump** is a vertical jump. An individual marks the full extent of their normal reach on a wall or vertical measuring board using a pen, and then tries to reach a point as far beyond the initial mark as possible using the power of their legs.

- **The standing long jump** is a horizontal jump. An individual stands at the edge of a horizontal measuring board and, with both feet together, jumps forward as far as they can.

Testing muscular endurance

- **The press-up test** – assesses the muscular endurance of the chest, shoulders and arms. The total number of press-ups completed in one minute is the score. Traditionally the press-ups for males and females differ as men should be in contact with the ground at their hands and toes while women should be in contact with the ground at their hands and knees or on a slightly raised bar. The resting position is up with elbows locked.

- **The sit-up test** – assesses the muscular endurance of the abdominals and hip flexors. The test usually measures the number of sit-ups completed in one minute.

Case study

The multi-stage fitness test (MSFT) involves continuous running between two markers 20 m apart in time with a set of pre-recorded bleeps. The start speed of this test is about 8 km/hr, which is really just a fast walk, but the length of time between the bleeps decreases every minute or every level. This means that running speed must increase by 0.5 km/hr each time the level changes if the individual is to keep time with the bleeps.

Scoring is based on the number of levels and shuttles completed, so for instance 7/2 means level 7 has been reached and 2 shuttles completed.

1 What do you think are the advantages of the MSFT?
2 Find out which services use this test as part of their selection process.
3 What score do you get on the MSFT?
4 Is your score good enough to get you into the service you would like to join? If not, what can you do to improve?

▶ Health tests

Another set of commonly-used health-related tests include body mass index (BMI) and body composition.

Body mass index (BMI) is a measure of whether a person is over or underweight. It is easily calculated using a simple formula. Multiply your height in metres by itself and then divide it by your weight in kilograms.

Worked example 5.1

A woman with a height of 1.6 m and a weight of 66 kg is working out her BMI.

$$\frac{66}{(1.6) \times (1.6)} = \frac{66}{2.56} = 25.8$$

This woman has a BMI of 25.8, which suggests that she is very slightly overweight.

A BMI of 18.5–24.9 is within the healthy range recommended by the NHS.

Activity 5.7 — Calculating BMI

Calculate your own BMI using the formula above. What does your BMI say about your level of health and fitness?

The woman in Worked example 5.1 would like to bring her BMI down into the normal range, but she does not do much exercise. What could you suggest she does to achieve her goal?

? Did you know?

- A BMI below 18.5 would be considered underweight.
- A BMI of 18.5–24.9 is in the normal range.
- A BMI of 25–29.9 is considered overweight.
- A BMI of 30–39.9 classed as obese.
- A BMI of over 40 is very obese ('morbidly obese').

Body composition (or body fat percentage) is a measure of the amount of fat in a person's body. It is usually measured with skinfold callipers, although many gyms now assess it electronically with a device very similar to weighing scales, which measures electrical resistance in the body.

Callipers can be difficult to use accurately. Measurements are normally taken in four places:

- biceps
- triceps
- subscapula (below shoulder blade)
- suprailiac (just above waist).

The measurements in millimetres are then calculated to give a body fat percentage. A reading of 13–17% would be ideal in males aged 16–29, and 21–25% would be ideal for women aged 16–29.

▷ Public services requirements of test results

As you saw in Topic B.1 (pages 152–156), uniformed services use fitness tests as part of their selection process. These tests are used to ensure that:

- all new recruits start training with the same minimum standard level of fitness
- applicants have the necessary motivation to perform in the services
- applicants understand that fitness is important to the job
- applicants will be able to physically do the job they are applying for.

The fitness tests are carefully chosen to best represent the needs of each service and are often reviewed. These reviews can lead to changes so it is a good idea to keep up to date with the requirements of the service you wish to join.

Assessment activity 5.3 — Maths

Your personal performance in public service fitness tests will be key in enabling you to join the service of your choice. In order to see how physically ready you are for the challenges ahead, complete the following tasks.

- Participate in fitness tests for two different public services and maintain a logbook of your results.
- What do your results show about your performance?
- Are there any improvements that you can make?

Tips

- Consider how you can present the results of your fitness tests. Your logbook will show your test results, but you need to discuss what your results indicate about your performance. You could do this in the form of a short report or a verbal discussion with your tutor.
- Consider what your results tell you – what are your strengths and what do you need to improve? What sort of things could you do to improve?

WorkSpace

▶ Tasha Casimir

Personal trainer

After I completed my BTEC First in Public Services, I realised that I wanted to join the army as a fitness instructor. I was too young to join at the time, so I decided to complete a level 3 qualification in personal training and gain some experience working with clients before joining the army.

The job is really varied. I work at a private gym and I see all different types of clients, from people who haven't exercised in years and are very overweight, to people who are training for specific events such as marathons. It means I have to be able to understand the diet, nutrition, lifestyle and fitness requirements of people of all ages, genders and backgrounds.

I find that many people are scared of coming into a gym so, as well as helping them lose weight and get fitter, I also have to build their confidence and motivate them to continue.

The best part of the job is when I see a real physical and psychological difference in someone I have been training. They can seem like a new person: much happier and more confident.

I have been given my start date in the army now. I am really looking forward to getting through basic training and using my skills as part of the team that ensures the army is fit and ready for whatever faces it.

Think about it

1 Why is it useful to have spent some time working with the public before joining a service?

2 What advantages does working with a wide variety of clients have for Tasha?

3 What have you learned in this unit which will help you pass the fitness tests of your chosen service?

Unit 1: The Role and Work of the Public Services (page 41)

1 **A** and **C**

2 Possible answers include:

- refuse collection
- registration of births, deaths and marriages
- administration of social housing
- collection of council tax
- road maintenance
- any other relevant answers.

3 Possible responses/indicative content. Identification and discussion of services such as:

- the Ambulance Service – treatment of casualties, decontamination, major incident response
- the Police Service – crime scene protection and analysis, investigation and arrests, managing major incident scenes
- the local authority – funding allocations, setting of council tax levels, fire safety in premises
- the armed services – evacuation during major incidents or severe weather events. Accept any other relevant answers.

Disclaimer: These practice questions and sample answers are not actual exam questions. They are provided as a practice aid only and should not be assumed to reflect either the format or coverage of the real external test.

A

Anaemia – a lack of iron in the body, which makes you tired and pale.

Antenatal – before birth, or relating to pregnancy.

B

Bias – People often have strong opinions about certain topics. This is called 'bias'. Newspaper or magazine articles, or information found on the internet, may be biased to present a specific point of view.

Blue light services – the main emergency services: police, fire and rescue, ambulance and coastguard.

C

Cardiovascular – associated with blood flow and circulation. The cardiovascular system includes your heart and blood vessels.

Complement – add to something (such as a service) in a way which enhances it.

Custody – in the justice system, this means imprisonment.

D

Devolve – to transfer power from central government to regional government.

E

Endorphins – hormones released in the brain and nervous sytem.

Excise duty – a tax on the sale of goods within a country.

F

Fitness – your ability to perform a particular task or set of tasks. The level of fitness required for particular tasks will vary.

H

Halal – a halal diet abides by the principles of Islam and does not include alcohol, pork or pork products. Animals killed for meat must be killed in a particular way.

Hazard – a potential source of harm to a person or group of people.

Health – a state of physical and mental well-being where your body is free of disease and is working as it should.

Homophobia – an extreme and irrational dislike of homosexuality or homosexuals.

I

Icebreakers – activities which help introduce people and allow them to get to know each other.

Incident – anything that requires attention by the public services. It could be a fire, a serious motorway crash or a fight outside a pub.

Inheritance – the passing on of property, titles or money after someone has died.

Innovative – new or different ways of doing things.

Interdependence – relying on others and having them rely on you.

J

Jargon – this means words and phrases that are used specifically within an organisation, such as 'blues and twos' for the lights on police cars or 'fence' to describe a person to whom stolen goods are sold.

K

Kosher – a kosher diet abides by the principles of Judaism and does not include pork and pork products. Meat and dairy food should not be eaten together, and animals killed for meat must be killed in a particular way.

L

Legacy – an amount of money or property left to someone in a will.

Lethargy – feeling sluggish and lacking in energy.

Lifestyle – this is the way you choose to live your life. Lifestyle choices include factors such as your leisure activities, dress, diet and your personal relationships.

M

Metabolism – the rate at which you use the energy in the food you eat. Nutrients that are processed into energy are 'metabolised'.

N

Nutrition – the study of how the body uses foods and nutrients vital to health in the growth, maintenance and reproduction of cells.

O

Outsourcing – when a public service contracts a private company to provide a service on its behalf.

P

Paper sift – a way of removing unsuitable applications, used by many public services and other employers. It involves checking an application form and weeding out any forms that are incomplete, show a poor standard of English, or demonstrate that the individual is unsuitable for the job.

Parliament – the body of people and organisations which governs a country. In the UK, this is made up of the king or queen, the House of Commons and the House of Lords.

Plagiarism – If you are including other people's views, comments or opinions, or copying a diagram or table from another publication, you must state the source by including the name of the author or publication, or the web address. Failure to do this (so you are really pretending other people's work is your own) is known as plagiarism. Check your school's policy on plagiarism and copying.

Probation – this is the period of time after an offender is released, when they are supervised and must show good behaviour.

Prosecute – to carry out legal proceedings against someone.

Pulses – the edible seeds of certain plants. Lentils, peas and beans are pulses.

R

Regimental system – a way of organising a fighting force so that each soldier is recruited, trained and administered by the regiment in which they serve for their entire career. It creates intense loyalty to the regiment.

Remit – a task or set of jobs given to an individual or organisation.

Respiratory – associated with the intake and expiration of oxygen. The respiratory system includes your nose, mouth, larynx and lungs.

Risk – the likelihood that a person or group of people may be harmed by a hazard.

S

Scrutiny – the process of examining something very carefully.

Slang – words that we use informally (i.e. you and your friend/colleague may know what it means, but others would not).

Statutory – required by law. A statute is another name for a law or Act of Parliament.

Stereotypes – widely held views which present an oversimplified or generalised opinion.

Stimulant – a substance that raises the body's level of physiological or nervous activity.

SWOT analysis – a self-analysis technique in which you consider the Strengths, Weaknesses, Opportunities and Threats of a project or yourself.

T

Tender – a bid or proposal. It contains information on how a company would deliver the service being put out to tender and how much it would charge for doing this.

Third sector – another name for the voluntary sector.

Try – to put someone on trial.

Index